THE ACROPOLIS
AND ITS MUSEUM

CLIO EDITIONS

athens 1979

Translation: ALEXANDRA DOUMA

Art layout: RACHEL MISDRACHE-CAPON

Photographs: M. SKIADARESES, N. KONTOS, A. SPYROPOULOS

Colour separation: "EUROGRAPH"

Phototype-setting: FOTRON S.A.

Printed by: L KARYDAKIS., ATHENS

THE ACROPOLIS
AND ITS MUSEUM

GEORGE DONTAS: Director of the Acropolis
General Ephor of Antiquities

**Acropolis.
Signification;
the Athenian
acropolis of the
Mycenaean
period**

Acropolis means the highest part of the city. In ancient Greece which was divided into innumerable city-states, each of these had its own acropolis, a naturally fortified hill, reinforced with ramparts, used in cases of emergency as the ultimate refuge for the inhabitants of the region. The most famous of these, and rightly so, was the Acropolis of Athens which, in time, also monopolised the meaning of the word. Many acropoles had existed in Greece from prehistoric times and some of them such as Mycenae and Tiryns — the most important centres of one of the most splendid prehistoric civilisations, the Mycenaean (which took its name from Mycenae) — with their mighty ramparts built of enormous irregular boulders even today make a marked impression on those visiting them. Athens was also one of the centres of the Mycenaean world. Even though it was not as important as the cities of the NE Peloponnese it did, nevertheless, play a not insignificant role at the close of the Mycenaean period. The same time as the metropoles of the Mycenaean world were walled, the rocks of the Athenian Acropolis were also enclosed (13th century B.C.) by a similarly mighty, impressive rampart which subsequent tradition attributed to beings with supernatural strength, the Cyclops. Significant sectors of the fortification wall are still preserved today — the best-preserved is a portion behind the south wall of the Propylaia.

The acropoles of prehistoric times were something more than those of later times. They not only served as a place of refuge but, first and foremost, as the place of residence of the sovereign of the land, *Anax* as he is called in the Pylos tablets — the *king* as he was known later. The palace on the Athenian Acropolis was located somewhere towards its north side, either there where the Archaic temple of Athena was built later, or a little further east on the summit of the hill. Within the palace the great gods of the Mycenaean religion were worshipped with much ceremony, the omnipotent goddess of nature and fertility, the subsequent Athena, as well as the god who accompanied her, Erechtheus, in three phases, child, husband and dying. Many scholars maintain that the king himself had divine honours during his lifetime and after his death, that his palace was a shrine and for this reason the first temple was founded on this very site. But this is still a matter for conjecture. The most important event in the Late Mycenaean period in Athens was the amalgamation into a single city *(synoikismos)* which is traditionally attributed to Theseas, the apparently peaceful unification of Athens and the other city-states of Attica into a united state with equal rights and simply having the same seat of administration, Athens. Through the synoikismos the new country accrued considerable economic and political power.

**The Acropolis in
the Dark Ages
(end of 2nd,
beginning of 1st
millennium B.C.)**

The transformation of the Acropolis from the political and military centre it was into an exclusively cult site was allied to the immense changes which took place within the Greek area at the end of the 2nd millennium B.C. Primitive peoples, not foreigners however, devastated the centres of the Mycenaean civilisation in the 12th century, they captured the acropoles one after another and plunged the country into anarchy. Panic-stricken populations fled in all directions seeking salvation and new patriae, the civilisation was obliterated or at least devolved into a state of primitive society. The only state in Greece which escaped this destruction was Athens

1. A panoramic view of the Acropolis from the SW. The Parthenon stands in the centre.

2. The Acropolis from the W, as one sees it beyond the pines and cypresses of the hill of Philopappos.

3. A closer view of the Acropolis from the W. The Parthenon stands majestically in the middle, the complex of the Propylaia and the Nike temple on the left.

and Attica, the king of which, Kodros, was sacrificed, according to tradition of his own volition, fighting the enemy at the borders of his native land in order to save it from subjugation as some oracle had decreed. After Kodros' death a great change in the political life of Athens was initiated and eventually consummated. The authority which had been formerly concentrated in the hands of a hereditary sovereign was now shared among several men at the same time and for a short time. So, even though the social structure continued to be aristocratic the foundations of the subsequent democratic body politic were introduced. The new rulers, the *Aristoi* (excellent ones) as they were called, who were the wealthy land-owners, fearing the restoration of the monarchy, transferred the political centre from the rock to the lower city, to its northern foothills, there where, in the course of time, the *agora* developed. The Acropolis was given over to cult and did not become a fortress again until over 1000 years later at the close of antiquity.

During these dark ages at the beginning of the 1st millennium B.C. the stuff of oral tradition of prehistoric times, religious and historical, began to be crystallised into myths in which reality was interwoven with religion and cult to form a unity whose parts were difficult to distinguish. Athena or "Medeousa of Athens" was derived from the prehistoric goddess and gave her name to the city. She had two aspects. As one the protectress of the forces of the earth, of crops and of the fertility of mankind *(Polias),* as the other the war-loving

3

The oldest temple of Athena

patroness of the city and a virgin *(Pallas)*. From as early as Geometric times she was worshipped in a small temple situated to the south of the later Erechtheion. Her statue primitively fashioned from wood *(xóanon)* was believed by the Athenians to have fallen from heaven *(diipetés)*.

Homer even mentions the temple twice, on one occasion as the "wealthy temple" *«πίων νηός»* and the other as the "revered house of Erechtheus" *«Ἐρεχθῆος πυκινὸς δόμος»*. At some unspecified point in time, Erechtheus gave way to another god who took his place beside Athena, Poseidon. Poseidon was the god of earthquakes and the sea and was mainly worshipped by Ionian populations of the Peloponnese, he is even mentioned in the Pylos tablets. His entry into the religious firmament of Athens was rather late, either at the end of the 2nd millennium with the Neleis who settled in Athens as refugees from Pylos, or even later. His "intrusion" did not, however, take place unopposed as is evident from the myth of his quarrel with Athena. Its conclusion, however, as is well-known, was his reconciliation with the goddess and their cohabitation in the same temple, displacing Erechtheus. According to one tradition Poseidon slew Erechtheus with his trident. In any case, neither he nor Athena gave their name to the building which is named after Erechtheus. Around these myths are woven other myths and names such as Kekrops, mythical king of Athens who was half man (from the waist upwards) and half snake (from the waist down). The snake was the sacred animal of Erechtheus, and later also of Athena and according to tradition resided in her temple as the "household snake" *(oikouros ophis)*. In time the owl was also assigned to Athena in addition to the snake; the worship of the former was perhaps brought from Pylos by the Neleis.

First monumental building phase of the temple of Athena (7th century B.C.)

In the middle of the 7th century B.C., in many parts of Greece, monumental sculpture first appeared and, shortly afterwards, monumental architecture. Whence these tendencies initially stemmed which led rapidly to the unsurpassed grandeur of Greek art of the Archaic and Classical times is a puzzle which has occupied archaeologists for generations. Nevertheless, Athens was one of the first and most important centres of its development. Its significance as a city-state and its economic development which was barely affected by the acute social struggles of the 7th century B.C. was echoed by the floruit experienced in those years by the great sanctuary of the Acropolis and certain of its peripheral sanctuaries, e.g. the sanctuary of Poseidon at Sounion. Great Attic sculpture from this period has not survived except at Sounion. However, the first large building in Athens was built on the Acropolis. It replaced the small sanctuary of the Geometric period with new and, for the period, imposing dimensions, and for the first time the roof was pedimented (though only on the east side) and adorned with an extremely impressive sculpted composition, two lionesses killing two calves (one of them has survived — Museum).

Second monumental building phase of the temple now called the "Old Temple"

From the moment it took its first step towards the monumental dimension Greek art advanced continuously and at an ever-increasing pace from one conquest to another, from one evolutionary stage to the next. Not many decades elapsed (perhaps at the beginning of the 6th century B.C.) before the building had been radically renovated yet again and enlarged even more. By that time its greater part was of poros stone while sections of its roof were already of marble and a second pediment even existed, behind, as well as a small colonnade which surrounded the main building. It was then that alongside the traditional subjects of wrestling beasts others with a mythological content were introduced. The portrayal of myth which has as its source the pronouncedly anthropocentric conception of the Greek was an important innovation which decisively influenced the whole of subsequent art. This temple continued, despite all the alterations, to be called the "Old Temple", that is it was accorded the same treatment as the very ancient building which had first been erected on this site centuries before.

"Treasuries"

Somewhat later, in the second quarter of the 6th century, other smaller buildings were also built at various points in the sanctuary. Their function does not, however, seem to have been for worship, they served other needs. Some of them were perhaps Treasuries, similar to the small edifices known from other panhellenic sanctuaries in which sacred votives etc. were kept.

Votives

The first marble statues apparently appeared on the Acropolis at that time. The best-known of these, the so-called Moschophoros (Calf-bearer) was offered by a nobleman called Romvos, as we learn from the inscription engraved on its base. Statues and buildings are, in the main, votives of the wealthy aristocracy of the countryside, the *Pedieoi*, whose power was curtailed around the middle of the 6th century by a strong man, Peisistratos who exercised dictatorial control of the state, with a few interruptions, for a whole generation. Despite the arrogance of Peisistratos, his administration was not so much tyrannical as enlightened despotism which still formally respected the institutions. Above all, however, he promoted the economic development of the place to a considerable degree and reinforced Athens' political influence in the Greek world. When Peisistratos died in 527 B.C. his

Tyranny of Peisistratos

Tyranny of the Peisistratides

sons Hippias and Hipparchos continued to rule the city in the same way until 514 B.C. when Hipparchos was assassinated. His brother then became really violent and was overthrown in 511 B.C. In general, however, the era of the Peisistratides was one of great political and economic acme for Athens. One of their first tasks was, yet again, the renovation of the Old Temple of Polias Athena (circa 525 B.C.). The temple was rebuilt and although the supporting framework and other sections were of porous stone its pediments were of marble this time, likewise the metopes as well as other parts of it. The decoration on the west pediment was also innovative: For the first time myth dominated completely. A magnificent battle was depicted, the mythical Gigantomachy in which the patroness goddess, Athena, played a leading role.

Third building phase of the "Old Temple" (circa 525 B.C.)

This was the era when there was a sudden increase in the number of statues on the rock dedicated by the faithful to the goddess. The majority were in the form of maidens (the so-called *kores)* and exhibited an incredible, for the period, variety of faces and expressions (to such an extent that one is inclined to characterise them as the beginnings of portraits) as well as charming attitudes and elegant raiment on which the original colours are frequently preserved. This group of kores from the Acropolis has, justifiably, won world-wide acclamation.

Democracy (507 B.C.)

The overthrow of Hippias and the establishment of the democratic state in 507 B.C. did not interrupt the dedication of votives in the sanctuary of the rock which continued at the same rate. National opinion was directly bolstered immediately following the unprecedented victory of the Athenians over the Boiotians and Chalkidians during the very first year of the democracy. It was then that the city bound its enemy hostages in chains which were later dedicated on the Acropolis and from the tithe of the booty a chariot was made which was also dedicated to Athena. At the same time the miniscule temple was built in honour of Athena Nike in her very ancient sanctuary which was located beside the entrance to the Acropolis.

Birth of the Classical period

The serious events of the final decade of the 6th century matured not only the character of men but of art: The refreshing, carefree air of the Archaic statues thenceforh gave way to a gathering up which was not slow in becoming soul-searching and introspective. For the first time the works were aware of themselves. Perhaps it is no coincidence that tragedy was also coming to fruition during these years. The Classical period of Greek art chiefly stems from Athens.

Commencement of the building of the Parthenon after the Battle of Marathon (490 B.C.)

After the even more unexpected victory of the Athenians, with Miltiadhes as general, over the Persians at Marathon in 490 B.C. the youthful democracy decided to build next to the Old Temple of Athena Polias a splendid new temple which was to be dedicated to Pallas Athena. From then onwards Athena would make her presence felt to the citizens in her double aspect, as a pacific and a martial goddess.

It seems that the state also ordered, at the same time, the construction of a monumental propylon which would be worthy of the sanctuary.

Destruction of Athens and the Acropolis in 480 B.C.

Neither of these buildings was ever finished. In the summer of 480 B.C. the Persians captured Athens and its Acropolis and destroyed them. In the two years they remained in the land they completed the desolation by burning everything. So, when the Athenians returned victorious to their home the city and its great sanctuary as well as the countryside and all its sanctuaries were mounds of charred ruins. Inspired, however, by the victor of Salamis, Themistocles and the moderate politician Aristeides, the Athenians set to work immediately. The debris of the holy buildings and the votives of the Acropolis were carefully and probably with reverence placed like venerable

Return of the Athenians (478 B.C.). Walling of the city and north rampart of the Acropolis. Delian League

relics in hollows in the rock, thus protecting them, unwittingly, from future disasters and pillaging. To Themistocles the Athenians owed the implementation of a new fortification of their city which was hastily undertaken to face the possibility of another invasion from the Persians or other enemy as well as the building of Piraeus which was destined to play the role of the largest commercial and military harbour in the Mediterranean. To Aristeides they owed the organisation of the major alliance of insular and coastal cities of the Aegean, the so-called Delian League (from the island Delos which constituted until 454 B.C. its religious and fiscal centre) the aim of which was the continuation of the war against Persia, initially one of liberation, later taking the offensive. Athens held the leading position in the League and with her large navy and skilful army commander, Kimon, son of Miltiadhes, gained such decisive victories over the Persians which brought it immense economic benefits and ensured it first place among the cities of the Hellenic world.

Walling of the south rampart

Resumption of the building of the Parthenon

After the victory of Eurymedon river (468 B.C.) Kimon built, according to Plutarch's testimony, the south rampart of the Acropolis (as well as the Long Walls outside it which united Athens with the sea) like the north fortification wall which is usually considered to have been the work of Themistocles. It is also believed by many scholars that Kimon embarked on the construction (or reconstruction as we maintain) of the temple of Pallas Athena, known the world over as the Parthenon. An oath sworn by the Greeks before the battle of Plataiae decreed that no city should rebuild the sanctuaries which the Persians had destroyed so that their ruins would remain for all time a monument to the barbarity of the Persian invaders. However, it seems that practical reasons had necessitated the partial repair of the Old Temple on the Acropolis since within it, in accordance with a well-known Greek custom, the Athenians stored the money of their city. In the event that the building of the temple of Pallas Athena is considered a work of Kimon then one explanation may be given, the nationalistic fervour which overcame the Athenians after their great military victories and which assured them the dominant position they held in the Greek world.

Statue of Athena Promachos

Certainly the colossal bronze statue of Promachos Athena which was set up on the Acropolis can also be attributed to Kimon. According to tradition it was paid for from the booty of the battle of Marathon, more probably from the rich spoils of the battle of the river Eurymedon. Its artist was the Athenian sculptor Pheidias who gained great fame thanks to his work. The Athenians were to speak of this artist for many years to come.

Death of Kimon (450 B.C.). Democratic party (Pericles)

When Kimon died in 450 B.C. the power of the aristocratic party was reduced to nothing for a long period of time and the radical democratic party held sway. Its leader was a member of an old esteemed aristocratic family, Pericles, son of the general Xanthippos. Pericles changed both the foreign and the domestic policy. While the aristocratic party was expressly anti-Persian and pro-Spartan, the democratic one was neutral in its dealings with Persia. In its relations with Sparta, however, it was clearly hostile. Pericles envisaged not only a leading role for Athens in a large insular and Asia Minor alliance but the unification of the whole of Hellenism into one body under the hegemony of Athens. His vision was enterprising and hitherto unheard of in the Greek world. Many traditional Greek powers were suspicious and first and foremost, naturally, Sparta. The preconditions for its success were, however, favourable.

The city had tremendous political and intellectual influence and the impressive alliance furnished copious economic resources, the first time they

4. A further close-up view of the west side of the Acropolis. The complex of the Propylaia from which the little Nike temple can now be clearly distinguished to the right, on top of its tower. At the left edge the right tower of the Late Roman Beulé Gate.

Transfer of the Delian League under the hegemony of Athens

were so plenteous in the Greek world, derived from the tax paid by the allies to the exchequer on Delos. Nevertheless, there were many in Athens and elsewhere who asked: Was there any reason for the League's existence after the peace made with Persia? Yes, declared Pericles. It was the League which ensured peace in the Aegean, and first of all Athens and for this reason the cities would continue to pay their tax. So Athens was able to withdraw as much money as it wished from the treasury of the League in order to embellish the capital of the League with buildings the like of which had not been seen before in the Hellenic world. Magnificent buildings befitted the city which stood in the front line of hellenism and it was quite natural that the League should pay for them. The conservative and pro-Spartan citizens objected that the immense power and influence of Athens would be to the detriment of Sparta which was their paradigm. However, Pericles' dynamic personality prevailed, the radical patriot began to implement his programme in 450 B.C. — an inspired and of course costly project — which he had conceived of with certain of his friends, Aspasia, the sculptor Pheidias, the philosopher Anaxagoras et al. The buildings of the Acropolis were to be rebuilt on the basis of a uniform plan, nowadays this would be called town-planning, and

Pericles' programme for the beautification of the Acropolis by erecting new buildings

the dimensions of the buildings and their internal magnificence would exceed, under the influence, surely, of Pericles' friends in Asia Minor, everything then known to the civilisation of Mainland Greece. Even the implementation of the programme was undertaken by the best artists at the disposal of Athens and its League. An entire army — as Plutarch, Pericles' biographer so aptly described it later — was recruited for the task: architects, sculptors, bronze-casters, gold-smiths, painters as well as merchants and sailors and every kind of artisan and many more. The "army", however, required a commander so that each member could find his "rank" in it. This was Pheidias whom Pericles appointed as general supervisor of his works. *"All was managed by the overseer of everything, Pheidias friend of Pericles."* He admired, says Plutarch, the speed with which the works of Pericles were erected one after the other, particularly since this speed did not adversely affect the value of the works. On the contrary, they were made in a "short time" for "all time" because: *"Each one of them, in its beauty, was even then and at once antique; but in the freshness of its vigour it is, even to the present day, recent and newly wrought. Such is the bloom of perpetual newness, as it were, upon these works of his, which makes them ever to look untouched by time, though the unfaltering breath of an ageless spirit has been infused into them".*

Pheidias

The buildings of the Periclean programme

The Parthenon, Odeion, Long Walls, Telesterion at Eleusis, Propylaia are referred to by Plutarch as works of Pericles though archaeological scholarship has added others to the list such as the temple of Hephaistos in the Agora ("Theseion"), the temple of Ares at Acharnes (which under Augustus was dismantled and also removed to the agora), the temple of Poseidon at Sounion and others. Perhaps never again would mankind see such concentrated artistic production of such a high quality executed in such a short space of time. In the same era a host of splendid votive sculptures was set up on the Acropolis and in other sanctuaries and areas of the city and of Attica, creations in bronze or marble of the greatest artists known in antiquity.

The Peloponnesian War of 431 B.C. suddenly interrupted this flood of creativity. It only awaited the slightest opportunity to be expressed again. This was provided by the Peace of Nikias (421-415 B.C.). It was then that the Nike temple was built and that construction of the Erechtheion commenced, the Asklepieion etc. was first established beneath the Acropolis. A further interruption on account of the Sicilian Campaign which ended in disaster (413 B.C.) and a new sortie with the first favourable breeze (410 B.C.) the completion of the Erechtheion and a few secondary buildings on the Acropolis. The Classical Acropolis was completed when, in the 5th century B.C., it met its well-known tragic end with the nightmarish occupation of the city by its rivals and the imposition of tyranny.

The city and the Acropolis in the later centuries of antiquity

At the beginning of the 4th century Athens, where democracy had meanwhile been restored, recovered remarkably quickly from the heavy blow of its defeat, it formed a new alliance, it struggled to play yet again the role of a great power. However, history then turned its attention elsewhere, to the fresh and vigorous power of Macedonia. Although the artistic production and intellectual life of Athens continued to be lively the city was slowly but surely immersed into spiritual narcissism and reminiscence of its former grandeur. One could say that by now the bone was missing from its ever softening flesh. On the Acropolis the votives multiplied but very few buildings were added and the area, moreover, had been considerably narrowed. The stage of history changed with the conquests of Alexander and the Eastwards expansion of

Hellenism, the Acropolis, however, changed very little. Eumenes II king of Pergamon accepted a votive four-horse chariot (quadriga) upon a high pedestal, almost attached to the Pinakotheke of the Propylaia (known as the pedestal of Agrippas) and an echo of the momentous events in the East is conveyed in the sanctuary with the well-known sculpted composition of the Galatomachy which his successor Attalos II offered upon the south rampart.

Roman period

A century and a half later the stage of history shifted once more, this time more fundamentally. Then it was that the West set out triumphantly on its path, Rome was mistress of the world. To the deified Rome and the Emperor Augustus the Athenians consecrated an elegant circular *monopteros* (without cella) temple, to the east of the Parthenon, inspired by the Erechtheion in its details. Some of the Roman emperors showed respect and even love for Athens and the Acropolis, Claudius for instance built the monumental staircase in front of the Propylaia. But outstanding among all was Hadrian who repaired the Parthenon which had been damaged by fire and built in the lower city a series of impressive buildings such as the Library, the Pantheon, the aqueduct et al. and finished the enormous temple of Olympian Zeus which had been begun some 600 years earlier by the sons of Peisistratos. Naturally, the Athenians responded to his benefactions with a host of commemorative portrait stratues which they set up both on the Acropolis and wherever else was convenient.

The catastrophic incursion of the Herouloi in 267 B.C.

A great disaster struck like lightning in 267 A.D. In those days the Roman state was ravaged by Civil Wars and devastated by foreign incursions. Forcing their way across the Straits of the Bosphoros and the Hellespont, the Teutonic hordes of Herouloi crossed the Aegean, reached Piraeus and attacked Athens. They sacked it mercilessly. It is an open question as to whether the Acropolis survived this invasion but even if it did hold out for a short time (the barbarians were quickly expelled by the Athenians under the leadership of the historic Dexippos) in the lower city, literally, not a single stone was left standing. According to a contemporary version the Herouloi also ascended the Acropolis which, of course, suffered from their looting and destruction, but this version is doubted. The wound was virtually mortal for Athens and the city was confined behind the so-called "Valerian Wall" which was built in a makeshift fashion from the ruins of the buildings which had been laid waste, and only extended over a part of present-day Plaka. For several decades

Recovery of the city from the 4th century A.D.

Athens remained a small town. However, in the fourth century its recovery began and was accompanied by a flourishing of its philosophical schools in which pagans and Christians studied together, such as Julian, later emperor, known as the Apostate, Basil the Great, Gregorios the Nazianzenos and many others. When, in circa 400 A.D., Eudoxia the Athenian acceded to the throne of Byzantium as the wife of the emperor Theodosius II she helped her birth-place, endowing it with splendid buildings outside the poor limits of the Valerian Wall e.g. the Gymnasium of the Agora, the Neoplatonic school which was discovered a few years ago to the south of the Acropolis etc.

However, the closing of the schools by Justinian in 529 A.D. was a most decisive blow even though it did not make quite the same impression as the destruction of the Herouloi. The philosophers left the city and it became a small provincial town. Eventually Christianity was imposed. The Parthenon became a church of Aghia Sophia (Divine Wisdom) and the Erechtheion too became a church though it is not known to whom it was dedicated. And later

Conversion of the temples into churches

Slavs and Saracens came to Athens and plunged the city into many centuries of oblivion.

**Medieval
Acropolis**

In around 1000 A.D. it was roused from its lethargy by an imperial visit. Basil II came to the city on his return as victor from the long-drawn-out campaign against the Bulgars and paid homage to the Virgin in the Parthenon, offering her a large precious kandela and repaired the building, embellishing it with wall-paintings. For almost two centuries Athens lived an intensive renaissance which the numerous churches and chapels which have survived from that period testify and which must have been even grander if we take into account the scores of other churches which have since disappeared. The last Metropolitan of Athens, before the city was captured by the Franks, Michael Akominatos was a learned man, no less erudite than those at the capital of the empire. When the Franks ruled Athens in 1205 and the Dukes de la Roche established their seat there, the Acropolis became a fortress once again after 2000 years. The palace of the Dukes de la Roche was installed in the Propylaia which were rearranged for this purpose, banquets were organised in the Pinakotheke according to the knightly custom of the West. At the SW corner of the building a tall tower for reconnoitering the region, well-known as the Koulas, was built. It was demolished only about 100 years ago. The Parthenon was at that time the cathedral church (Notre Dame d' Athènes) and Latin priests celebrated the Mass according to the precepts of the Catholic church. The Parthenon remained a catholic church after the capture of Athens by the Catalans who vanquished the Franks at Kopaïs in 1311 and after the capture of the Acropolis and Athens by the Florentine merchants, Accajioli, from 1387 to 1456 when Athens was taken by the Ottoman army under Omar Turachan, general of Mohammed the Besieger, and the Turks turned it into a mosque. The first centuries of Ottoman rule passed by in darkness and silence. Very few European travellers visited Athens. The Erechtheion was converted into the harem of the Turkish commander (Disdare). In the 17th century, it is not known exactly when, either in 1640 or 1656, part of the Propylaia was blown up either struck by lightning or due to the explosion of a shell. During this century contacts with the West increased. An important event was the lavish visit of the French Marquis de Nointel whom the Roi-Soleil, Louis XIV, had sent as ambassador to the Sublime Porte. De Nointel came to Athens with a large retinue in 1674. Among his entourage was a painter, Carrey, otherwise a nonentity, who nonetheless became famous because on de Nointel's orders he made detailed drawings of the ancient monuments of Athens and in particular the Parthenon. Carrey's sketches are of inestimable value since they provide detailed pictures of the monument as it was at the final moment before its destruction. For only 13 years later the Venetian army under general Morosini, having come from the Peloponnese which it had meanwhile captured, besieged the Acropolis and considerably harassed the Turks with concentrated artillery fire. One of the shells fell on the Parthenon which was being used, on account of the circumstances, as a powder magazine and caused its explosion and the blowing up of the building, large sections of which were destroyed or hurled round about with great violence and even landed outside the rock. The force of the blast was such that the Turks were so alarmed they surrendered. The Venetians entered the Acropolis. Morosini then attempted to remove some of the sculptures of the Parthenon which were still in position but achieved very little and caused a great deal of damage. Furthermore, his stay in Athens, the "European Spring" of the Turkish occupied city only lasted for a few months. The following year Morosini assessed the strategic conditions somewhat differently and abandoned Athens. Thus the destruction of this magnificent monument was not even beneficial in that it brought the deliverance of the population from the Turkish yoke, the day of liberation was to come much

**The Franks on
the Acropolis**

**Capture by the
Turks (1456)**

**The Parthenon a
Muslim mosque**

**Destruction of
the Parthenon
(1687)**

5. The Parthenon from the NW. The Greeks' strong feeling for plasticity which is also expressed in architecture has achieved, in the Parthenon, an admirable harmony of corporality and elasticity, of majestic simplicity and lightness.

5

later. Indeed, fear of Turkish reprisals forced the population to disperse throughout other regions, near and far. Slowly but surely, however, the Athenians, though by no means all, returned to Athens and submitted to their fate of bondage. The travellers ever increased in number. From copper engravings we have many views of Athens and the Acropolis which had been transformed into a veritable village. There were the dwellings of the members of the guard and their families. A small mosque was built inside the ruined Parthenon.

Elgin misappropriates the Parthenon sculptures and other antiquities and takes them to England (beginning of the 19th century)

At the beginning of the 19th century the theft of a greater part of the decoration of the Parthenon and other monuments of the Acropolis was carried out in a systematic manner. The miscreant was a diplomat and the misappropriation was covered by the authority of an official action, a permit from the Sultan. He was Thomas Bruce, Lord Elgin, ambassador of His Majesty the king of England at the Sublime Porte. Taking advantage of the political climate of the era and of his position he achieved the issuing of a firman which permitted him to remove from those lands subject to the suzereinty of the Sultan whatsoever antiquities he desired. Elgin was a man who knew what he wanted and, moreover, how to get it: one of his confidantes, the Italian artist Lugieri, settled in Athens during the final years of the 18th century and almost continuously for two decades removed from the monuments on the Acropolis and elsewhere, on Elgin's behalf, those antiquities he deemed worthy or capable of removal. The quantity he removed was enormous, their artistic value inestimable. The most beautiful sculptures ever produced by mankind and many others were purchased in 1815 by the British Museum for a sum which caused the protests of Elgin.

The Greek struggle for liberation (1821)

With the outbreak of the Revolution in 1821 some Athenians and peasants of the region liberated Athens from the Turks and after a relatively brief siege captured the Acropolis also. A few years later the situation was reversed. Then the Greeks were besieged on the Acropolis by a strong Turkish army under Kutache Pasha. The defence was determined and aided by both Greeks and Philhellenes who sped from elsewhere in an effort to break the cordon, but the besiegers were many and mighty. In these operations the monuments were damaged, especially the Erechtheion a part of which was destroyed. In the end the Acropolis was once more surrendered to the Turks (1827) just a few months before the unforseen favourable change which brought the war to an end with the naval battle of Navarino. The Turks, however, remained on the Acropolis for several years and only left in 1833.

The Acropolis after the liberation

When Athens was declared capital of the new Greek state the rock was handed over into its protection. The ruins were cleared, the Turkish fortification of the Propylaia was dismantled, the Nike temple was reerected, some restoration work was undertaken on the monuments, especially the Parthenon and the Erechtheion (on which the stolen Karyatide was replaced and one of the others from which pieces were missing was completed). Just after the middle of the century the building of a museum was considered. For this purpose a relatively non-visible low area in the SE corner of the surface of the rock of the Acropolis was chosen. In the 1880's the Ephor of Antiquities P. Kavvadhias with the German architect Kawerau undertook a large excavation in the embankment of the Acropolis down to bed-rock. These brought to light the host of works of Archaic sculpture and architecture which had been destroyed in 480 B.C. by the Persians. Their vivid colours and the youthful freshness of expression of the statues astonished both specialists and laymen throughout the world and toppled the hitherto prevailing Classicistic conceptions concerning ancient art. The works thronged the museum. While a smaller building next to it housed the secondary works, the museum proper housed, of necessity closely packed together, the major works.

Restorations

An earthquake in 1894 brought to a head the question of restoration of the monuments which had been decided upon on the recommendation of an international committee of scholars. From 1898 onwards large-scale restoration works on the Acropolis were embarked on which lasted, almost without a break, until the Second World War. The appearance of the Parthenon, Propylaia, Erechtheion was significantly altered by these works in comparison with what it was in the 19th century. The Nike temple, because it had apparently been incorrectly restored and because the tower exhibited static weakness, was again demolished together with its tower. These works afforded the opportunity for an excavation of the tower's interior which resulted in the discovery of an Archaic sanctuary as well as of earlier prehistoric remains. The Acropolis was not damaged during the Second World War since Athens had been declared an undefended city. After the end of the war some further restoration works took place, the main one being the restoration and consolidation of the SE corner of the rampart behind the museum which showed signs of static weakness.

Present-day dangers to the monuments and the confrontation of them

But that which has increasingly preoccupied the Ephorate of Antiquities of the Acropolis has been the state of the marble of the monuments. The marble has suffered damage from two sides: On the one hand the expansion of the iron rods which the restorers had used to consolidate and join the members which they restored has caused breaching of the adjacent marble as a consequence of which pieces frequently fall, and on the other hand the disintegration of the outer layer of marble due to its conversion into gypsum as a consequence of the increase of sulphur in the atmosphere (from central heating, factories etc.) which reacts with water to form sulphurous acid. The first threat has been partially dealt with by the Ephorate for many years, with its limited resources, by removing the iron where possible and replacing it with bronze. But neither was it in a position to replace the large pieces of iron, nor, of course, could it combat the chemical erosion. So in 1975 the Ministry of Culture decided to establish a Working Party to study the problems and ways of treating the monuments of the Acropolis. It consists of specialised scientists and ministerial representatives who began their study with the Erechtheion which presented the widest range of problems and the most urgent need for measures to be taken. Its work, which concerns the south wall of the Erechtheion along with the Karyatides and the west wall of the building, has been published in a voluminous tome. The Archaeological Council has adopted the proposal of the Working Party, which was also discussed at an international meeting held in December 1977 in Athens, and decided to replace, at the earliest opportunity, the Karyatides with replicas and remove the originals to the Acropolis Museum.

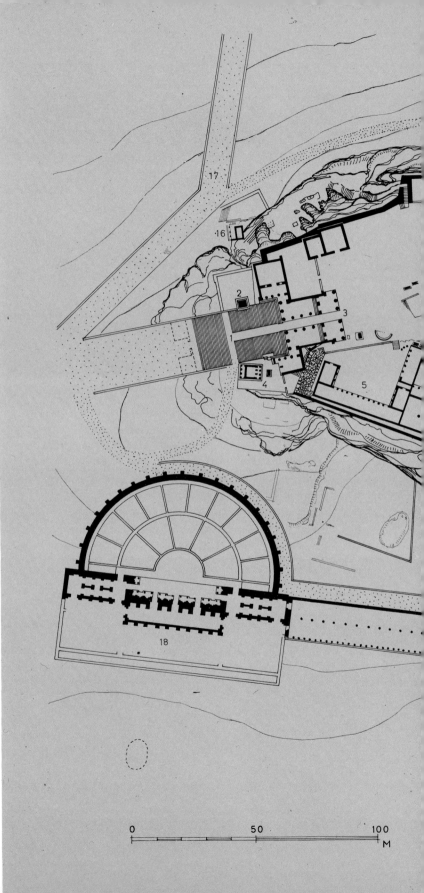

6. Plan of the
Acropolis and
immediate environs
(drawing by
J. Travlos). Legend:
1. Approach of
Classical times.
2. Pedestal of
Agrippa (earlier of
Eumenes II).
3. Propylaia.
4. Nike temple.
5. Brauroneion.
6. Chalkotheke.
7. Parthenon.
8. Temple of Roma
and Augustus.
9. Sanctuary of
Pandion.
10. Sanctuary of
Zeus Polieus.
11. Altar of Athena.
12. Erechtheion.
13. Pandroseion.
14. Arrephorion.
15. Statue of Athena
Promachos.
16. Klepsydra.
17. Panathenaic
Way.
18. Odeion of Herod
Atticus.
19. Stoa of
Eumenes.
20. Asklepieion.
21. Theatre of
Dionysos.
22. Later temple of
Dionysos.
23. Odeion of
Pericles.

0   50   100

M

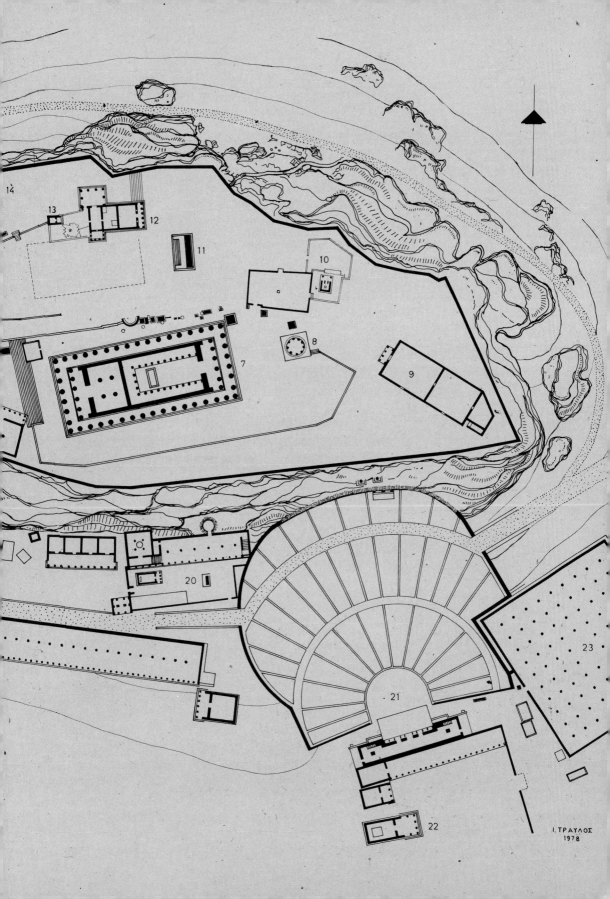

I. ΤΡΑΥΛΟΣ
1978

DESCRIPTION OF THE MONUMENTS

From reading the historical note it will have become clear that there were two periods of Athenian history which made a marked impression on the Acropolis: the Archaic (6th century B.C.) and the Classical (5th century B.C.). The monuments of the former were so completely destroyed by the Persian invaders in 480 B.C. that they are nowadays only revealed with difficulty. Only in the Archaic galleries of the Acropolis Museum is one able to see certain parts of them and experience the vitality and freshness of their expression. Conversely, the Classical monuments are spread out in their splendour across the entire surface of the rock, radiating even beyond into Athens which is spread all around, magnetising all who espy the Acropolis from afar, from the sea or the suburbs (that is as far as the endless concrete structures, which have relentlessly sprung up in the Attica basin during the last few decades, permit).

Beulé Gate

However, in order to reach the Classical monuments of the rock one must, inevitably, after ascending the west slope of the Acropolis, pass through a gateway from another era, the famous Beulé Gate which owes its name to the French archaeologist Beulé. It was he who, in the middle of the last century, revealed it together with its flanking towers, from the huge embankments which covered them. Built in make-shift fashion from members from buildings of the Classical period, mainly from buildings on the south slope of the Acropolis, this complex belonged to a major fortification of the Late Roman period (3rd century A.D.) which was designed, as I have said above, to protect the Acropolis from barbarian incursions which, in those days, wrought considerable damage.

Propylaia

As soon, however, as we cross the gate and are confronted high above by the complex of the Propylaia, entirely of white Pentelic marble, which impressively crown the summit of the sheer slope, with the airy little Nike temple, perched on the bastion which completes it, on their right, we immediately breathe in the air of the 5th century. The Propylaia were not only the monumental arrangement of the entrance to the sanctuary, they were also an invitation for the visitors to it. It is quite obvious that their form, a central building with two wings projecting westwards, was made to impress, even from a distance, the visitor who climbed up to them, to entice him and finally embrace him. In days gone by their enchantment was even more pronounced since the access was not known in detail but clear in general outline — it reached far below the Beulé Gate, extending for almost 80 metres in all. The Romans (under the Emperor Claudius in the middle of the 1st century A.D.) emphasised the access even further by covering it right to the top with a staircase of theatrical grandeur. However, the intention of making a theatrical impression was already in the mind of the architect of the Propylaia — Mnesicles according to the ancient sources — who must also have been responsible for the approach. Work on the building lasted for a comparatively short time. It commenced in 438 B.C., immediately after the completion of the Parthenon, and was interrupted in 432 B.C. shortly before the building was finished, most probably because of the imminent Peloponnesian War, which gloomy prospect imposed a cut in expenditure. The interruption did not mean, however, that the edifice remained half-finished. That which was not completed was the final working of some of the stones, to which the ancient Greeks paid particular attention. Thus, for example, the "bosses" were not

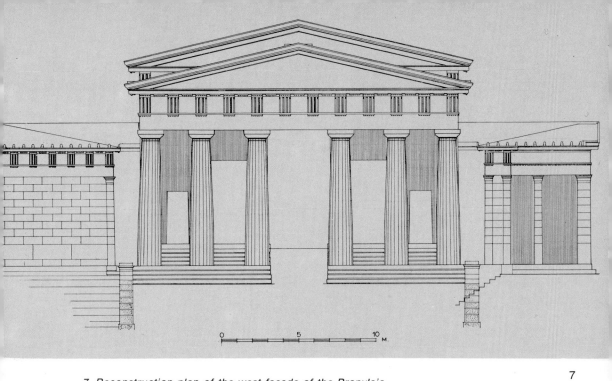

7. *Reconstruction plan of the west façade of the Propylaia.*

8. *The W façade of the Propylaia as it is today, seen from the Beulé Gate in the afternoon.*

7

8

9. The entire W front of the Acropolis.

10. Part of the W façade of the Propylaia and the Nike temple on its tower.

11. Section of the Propylaia, the east wall of the so-called Pinakotheke. The protruding "knobs" are ancient. The beam-rests and openings derive from Frankish works when the building served as the palace of the overlords.

12. From the central section of the Propylaia. On the left one of the Ionic columns springs up. The roof with its large beams can also be distinguished.

chipped off, principally on the outer side of the NE wall, as well as the final covering of marble in the right alcove of the west stoa.

In this very alcove, however, those sections which underwent the final "finishing off" still display the freshness, the extraordinary finesse of craftsmanship which achieved the annihilation of the joins between the stones and the smoothing of the surface so that it appears as a single piece.

Doric and Ionic order

The façades of both the central building and the wings are embellished with Doric stoas. Even though Athens was an Ionic place, the Athenians almost exclusively employed the Doric order until the middle of the 5th century B.C. More than the difference in their tribal origin, of which they were not particularly conscious anyway prior to the conflict between Athens and Sparta during the 5th century B.C., the exclusive use of the Doric order by the Athenians was due to their community with the other peoples of the Greek Mainland, where the Doric order was born and prevailed. For the Greeks of the mainland the Doric order was an expression of their architectural idiosyncracy. The clear-cut division of architectural members into 'supporters' and 'supported', the "entasis" exhibited by the supporting members striving to bear the weight of the supported ones, the accentuating of their mutual influence and their balanced composition, indicate the same passion in the stone as the mainland Greeks had for the well-exercised male body as well as for clarity of thought and moderated speech. Born further east, in the islands of the Aegean and on the Asia Minor coast, the Ionic order with its love of the "feminine" as is observable in the decoration on the capital and base, the virtually non-existent "entasis", the generally serene and soft expression, remained alien to the heart of the Athenians for several centuries. And when Pericles introduced it to Attic architecture in the middle of the 5th century B.C. he did so mainly to extol the common racial links between the Athenians and their allies. Indeed, initially the new order was employed cautiously and discreetly. In the Parthenon, for example, as we shall see later, only four of the columns are Ionic and these stand inside the building. The same applies to the Propylaia where the columns are situated in the interior of the central building, there are 6 in two rows of 3 each which divide the west wing of the central building into three aisles. Because of the large opening of the roof, supports were required to maintain it. Of these columns one, restored by Balanos, is to be marvelled at for the daring thrust right up to the roof.

NW wing of the Propylaia (Pinakotheke)

Of the wings of the Propylaia one, the NW, which was larger than the other, the SW, was decorated with painted compositions on the walls, most probably hanging pictures, and for this reason it has customarily been called the Pinakotheke. Recently the view has been expressed that some of the visitors to the Acropolis were received there and that there were couches aligned all around the walls, something like the so-called "Lesche" of the Knidians at Delphi.

Pedestal of the monument of Agrippa

In front of the NW edge of the Propylaia stands a tall pedestal of greyish-blue Hymettan marble — at one time it bore a bronze four-horse chariot driven initially by the king of Pergamon Eumenes II and later by the son-in-law of the Roman Emperor Augustus, Agrippa. The *Pedestal of Agrippa* considerably detracts from the spectacular Propylaia by the incongruity of its position and its cold colour.

SW wing of the Propylaia

The SW wing of the Propylaia is much smaller than the other, it consists only of a single stoa intended merely to comprise the architectural correspondent of the NW wing. The diminution in size was probably due to the proximity of the sanctuary of Athena Nike which obstructed an extension of

13. Reconstruction plan of the earlier propylon (according to Stevens). The zig-zag approach is not correct (for those times).

14. Reconstruction plan of the inside of the Acropolis through the Propylaia. The type of Athena Promachos was not the same as that depicted.

the Propylaia at the expense of its shrine. That a problem of boundaries existed is apparent from the fact that the Propylaia occupied space belonging to the Nike sanctuary on its NE side. Here a small staircase opened into the isodomic wall of the Nike Tower allowed the visitor direct access to the Nike sanctuary from the approach road without having to traverse the Propylaia.

The main building is not uniform. It consists of two sections, a larger west one which is at a slightly lower level and a smaller east one which is a few steps higher up. Externally this division of the central building into two sections was indicated by two different roofs. Of these two sections the larger west one, as we have said already, was separated by two rows of Ionic columns into three aisles because of the large opening of its roof. The east one was a simple stoa with a façade towards the sanctuary.

The sections were separated internally by five portals which were also the true boundary of the sanctuary. The middle one was the largest and the lateral ones decreased in size graduatedly towards the outer edges.

The Propylaia had no plastic decoration. An edifice whose purpose was basically functional had no need of the mythical word to be of significance, particularly since the creators of this period were especially careful in their use of descriptive means.

For the visitor whose main aim is to comprehend the wondrous monumental wealth of antiquity the subsequent history of the building is of very little interest. Therefore I refer to it here in a very few words just to complete the historical picture of the site, to bridge the ancient with the modern. In the Early Christian era a small church was built in a section of the building; the Frankish Dukes of Athens used the building as their palace and converted the Pinakotheke into a two-storeyed reception chamber. They also, probably, built a tall look-out tower at its SW corner (the so-called koulas). Lightning which struck a store of gun-powder (or bombardment) blew up the building in the middle of the 17th century, and its ruins were incorporated within a Turkish fortification wall which reinforced the defences of the Acropolis a few years later. The new Greek state cleared the building of this rampart, and the koulas was demolished in 1874. Between 1909 and 1917 a part of the building was restored by Balanos.

Sanctuary of Athena Nike

There had been a Nike sanctuary from earliest, indeed prehistoric times. Its existence beside the entrance to the Acropolis was exploited, it protected the rock's most vulnerable point from enemy incursions. This, perhaps, explains the cult of a martial goddess who ensured the efficacy of defence. Slowly but surely, as the centuries passed, this goddess was fused with Athena who was worshipped a little further off, on the top of the rock. When, just before the last World War, it was necessary to consolidate the tower which had signs of static weakness, in order to restore it it first had to be totally demolished, excavations were then carried out in the embankment inside and it was then discovered just how ancient the cult was and its phases were confirmed. It was an eschar at first into which, apart from the offerings to the dead, primitive figurines of the worshipped divinity were thrown; a

Archaic "oikos" of Nike

miniscule building with an altar before it in the middle of the 6th century B.C. was the precursor of the Classical temple. These were destroyed, like everything else, by the Persians. Shortly after the middle of the 5th century B.C. it was decided to repair the temple. However, work was delayed almost immediately when Pericles began implementing his building programme. This was not the time for small, traditional shrines, the grandiose, impressive buildings, those intended to laud the magnificence of the city, had precedence. Perhaps only the tower was constructed then and that only because it comprised part of the construction programme for the Propylaia. The temple's hour came a generation later, during the so-called Peace of Nikias (421-415 B.C.) the brief but fertile pause in the bloody Peloponnesian War. A new tiny temple and a marble parapet all around the tower with relief representations of Nikes and Athena was built. Even though in later years the goddess worshipped here continued to be called Wingless Nike (Victory) (because her statue was without wings) in Classical times, at least, the goddess was known as Athena Nike. This very elegant little temple is so graceful that the epithet Wingless Nike is eminently suitable. Work of a harsh era in ancient Greek history, this tiny temple may be interpreted as an expression of the dialectic of history, a stone flower which blossomed forth from the mud and blood of the fratricidal conflict.

Classical Nike temple, Kallikrates

In the Ionic order, since, for as long as the war with Sparta dragged on the Athenians increasingly emphasised their Ionic origins. There are four columns on its façade and four on its back face which is blind but turned towards the entrance to the Acropolis. An insular and Attic adaptation of the Ionic order was the use of a frieze which encircled the building above the epistyle (the Ionic buildings of Asia Minor do not have a frieze). On three sides, the N, W and S, (only a small fragment of the N one is original, all the rest are copies of the originals which are in the British Museum) battles are depicted, and on the entrance side a company of gods is shown (all originals). The cult statue was a "xoanon", that is of wood and very old, its type known from descriptions. Many of the plaques from the marble parapet are in the Acropolis Museum. Pieces of the altar have fallen down near the SW wing of the Propylaia.

The later history of the temple is in a few words: The building was taken to pieces bit by bit by the Turks in 1687 who used its material to reinforce the bulwark they were building to protect the west slope of the Acropolis; the temple was reconstructed in 1834-1838 by Ross, Schaubert and Hansen when the Turkish fortification was dismantled. The tower and temple were demolished and rebuilt between 1935 and 1940.

Mycenaean rampart ("Cyclopean")

Opposite the Nike temple, with the Parthenon in the background, we see an impressive section of the Mycenaean fortification wall. The ancient Greeks attributed it to the mythical Cyclops. It is 5 metres thick and constructed in a manner completely different from the classical one. Massive polygonal stones, the interstices filled with smaller equally irregular stones, conjure a picture of the turbulent, war-like conditions of that far-off era, the end of the Mycenaean period, when primitive tribes sought to topple the illustrious Mycenaean civilisation. They are a testimony of technical abilities exceptionally well-developed even by today's standards.

The interior of the Acropolis

Pausanias expressly says, when describing the Nike sanctuary, that from this site one could view the sea. Presumably because it was not visible from any other spot on the Acropolis. Nowadays, of course, things have changed and the whole of the Acropolis is exposed to the surrounding region, the distant mountains and the sea, thus reverting, in a way, to what it was of old, the summit of a rocky outcrop. However, in historical antiquity high ramparts prevented the visitor from looking outside, thus confining his view to the interior which, as an American archaeologist has aptly remarked, resembled an internal courtyard. If the extent of this surface now seems more than sufficient for the visitor to stroll about on this was not so in other times. To the aesthetic impression of narrowness given by the fortification walls was added an actual narrowness due to the presence of other buildings (apart from those

15. Reconstruction plan of the Brauroneion (first phase) (after Stevens).

which have survived) which have subsequently disappeared, plus a host of 'ex-votos' both large and small, which have also vanished. Completing the observation of the American archaeologist, we could characterise the inside of the Acropolis in ancient times as an open-air museum, indeed one of the richest and most exclusive in antiquity. Not only the few buildings which have survived but also many of the 'ex-votos' which have been lost were masterpieces of the artistic genius of the ancient Greeks. The visitor could, on traversing the Propylaia and proceeding further inside towards the altar of Athena which was usually his first objective, admire them from close at hand.

Panathenaic Way

The whole body politic passed by them in the course of the Panathenaia, the city's major festival, as the population streamed towards the "Old Temple" (later the Erechtheion) to offer the sacred peplos to the cult statue of the goddess (Panathenaic Way).

Statue of Athena Hygeia

One of the 'ex-votos' which has been lost, on its site, however, the signed base has been preserved, was attached to the SE column of the Propylaia. This was a bronze statue of Athena Hygieia (Health), work of the Athenian artist Pyrrhos, votive of the city following the great pestilence which brought it to its knees during the early years of the Peloponnesian War.

Brauroneion

Of the buildings which have disappeared also, the so-called Brauroneion was situated right next to the Panathenaic Way. This was the sanctuary of Brauronian Artemis, patron of pregnant and childbearing women, which housed the wooden cult statue (xoanon) of the goddess and the later marble statue of the same, work of Praxiteles. It was Π-shaped, open towards the Panathenaic Way. Beyond, to the east, was yet another building, this one in the form of a stoa, the Chalkotheke, in which, as its name suggests, (Greek chalkós = bronze), bronze vessels and 'ex-votos' were stored.

Parthenon

But the most important building on the sanctuary was, without doubt, the Parthenon. Formerly its size was diminished aesthetically by the buildings which surrounded it and also by the ramparts, today it dominates, unobstructed and freely in all directions. What does the name Parthenon mean? The virgin (parthénos in Greek) was, of course, Athena who, according to Athenian tradition stubbornly guarded her purity even when Hephaistos persistently pursued her. It is therefore obvious that Parthenon means temple or dwelling place of Athena Parthenos. This edifice is the crowning

16. The Nike temple from the east.

17. Reconstruction plan of the Nike temple.

18. The upper part of the E face of the Nike temple. The frieze is original.

19. The SW corner of the Parthenon with the only metope preserved 'in situ' on the S side.

achievement of Attic architecture and the most significant building of the Periclean programme. It was not, however, the first to be built on this spot. It was preceded, as we have said, in the historical note, by the temple begun by the Republic of Athens immediately following their victory at Marathon which perhaps also was intended to bear the same name. This pre-Persian temple also had significant dimensions, it was in fact larger than the Periclean one but not as wide. From its foundations which were not only retained but utilised by its glorious heir (the old foundation is visible today as a result of excavations conducted in the last century around its outside) it is evident that this early Parthenon was narrower than that of Pericles, for unlike the latter it did not have 8 columns on its narrow face, but only 6. This was formerly the rule for Doric temples. Even when Kimon started to rebuild the Parthenon he did not consider altering its design for, despite his audacious personality in questions of strategy, he was essentially deeply conservative. With Pericles, however, things were different. In spite of his aristocratic origin Pericles was a personality with wide horizons. He envisaged the Acropolis more as a political monument, a symbol of the great and prosperous Athens of his era, which would sing the praises not only of Athena and the city but of Hellenism in general. And even, of course, very discreetly — his role in building the new era of which he dreamt and which (to use a term of later European intellectualism) was the era of Athenian Enlightenment. He harnessed all means at his disposal, the advanced, for the time, science of geometry, the flourishing arts of all categories and the exceptional artists to realise his vision.

Architects of the Parthenon, Iktinos and Kallikrates. The role of Pheidias

Iktinos and Kallikrates are mentioned as the architects of the temple, the former is also known from the temple of Epikoureios Apollo at Bassae in Phygaleia, the latter from the little temple of Athena Nike. However, the true creator was someone else. Plutarch mentions as "controlling everything and supervisor of all", Pheidias. Even though not explicitly spoken of the real inspiration of the Parthenon seems to have been Pheidias, the most dynamic and multi-faceted artistic figure of the 5th century B.C. whose grandeur was extoled by the ancient Greeks. On viewing the Parthenon which is not only very long but very wide so that it spreads out majestically, it impresses, we feel the overwhelming spirit, the modesty and greatness and eternally acknowledged value of its art. Eight columns were required to support its width on the narrow sides, while there were seventeen on its long ones, that is a slight reduction in length compared with that of the preceding Parthenon which was a consequence of the desire for a perfect ratio of length to width which is here 9:4.

The "refinements" of the Parthenon

However, that which betrays the genius of its creator, that which fills even the hurried or cursory visitor with admiration are the so-called 'refinements' of the Parthenon which were adapted for such a large building in such a discreet and deeply harmonic combination. What are the 'refinements'? This term was coined by the Englishman Pennethorne, who first noticed them during the last century, to denote a host of deviations from the strict mathematical forms and whose purpose was to instill the pulse of life into an architectural body. I am not qualified to give an account of these endless 'refinements' in a brief guide to the Acropolis such as this is, but merely a partial and more generalised description of their extent and significance. The best-known are the so-called *'curves'*, that is the curvatures displayed by all the horizontal members of the building, from the foundation to the cornice. Their realisation required, as is understandable, a very high level of calculation and craftsmanship. Through them the creator infused the building with the breath of life, imparts the spirit of existence, challenges the

20. The Parthenon from NW. The three statues of the W pediment nowadays are copies of the originals which are in the Acropolis Museum. The metopes we see are all original.

21. Slab from the north frieze of the Parthenon. Horsemen. No. 863.

22. Slab from the south frieze of the Parthenon. Horsemen. No. 868.

23. Slab from the north frieze of the Parthenon. Apobates. No. 872.

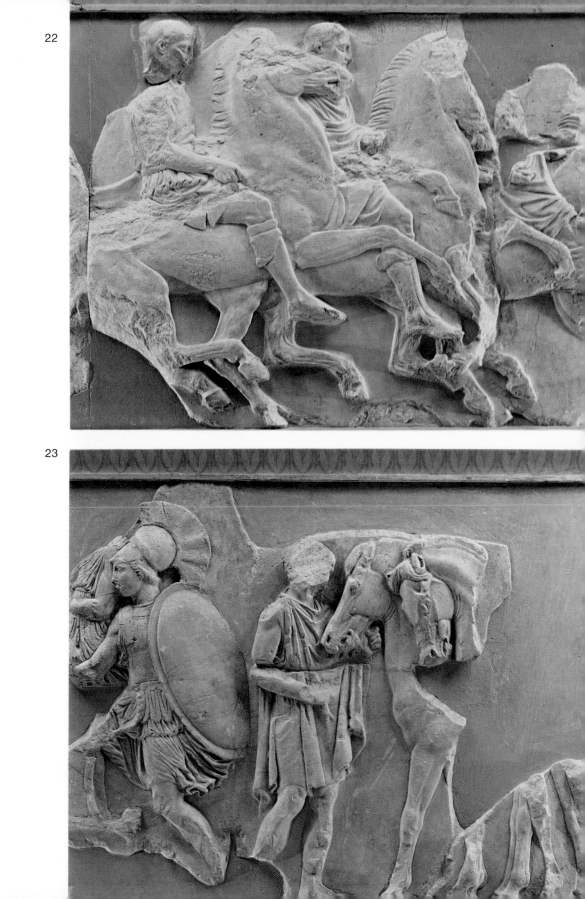

PLEASE DO NOT TOUCH
PRIÈRE DE NE PAS TOUCHER
BITTE NICHT BERÜHREN
SI PREGA DI NON TOCCARE

24. *The superb head of a horse of Selene's chariot at the north end of the east pediment of the Parthenon. British Museum.*

25. *Slab from the west frieze of the Parthenon. Young horsemen. British Museum.*

26. *Slab from the north frieze of the Parthenon. Youths ready to mount. British Museum.*

27. Metope from the south side of the Parthenon. Fight between a Lapith and a centaur. British Museum.

28. Slab from the north frieze of the Parthenon. Young horsemen. British Museum.

29. Slab from the north frieze of the Parthenon. Young horsemen. British Museum.

28

29

30

30. Group of two seated goddesses from the south edge of the east pediment: Demetre and Persephone. British Museum.

31. Group of two goddesses from the north end of the east pediment: Dione and Aphrodite? British Museum.

32. Body of a female deity running to the left from the west pediment of the Parthenon (Iris?). British Museum.

31

33. Section of the W frieze of the Parthenon seen between the columns of the W colonnade. The W frieze is the only one 'in situ' on the building.

34. Wide-angle photograph of the W face of the Parthenon. We see the frieze behind the colonnade on the exterior of the temple proper and the metopes between the triglyphs on the façade.

dead silence of the material and even the transcience of time.

The basic refinements of the columns are "diminution" *(meiosis)* and "swelling" *(entasis)*. The former is the slimming off of each column towards the top, the latter is the opposite tendency observed on each column, its swelling out at approximately ⅓ of the way up. More simplistically, *entasis* may be described as a reduction in the diminution along a certain section of its course, in the language of geometry it may be said to constitute, together with diminution, part of a parabolic curve. As far as art is concerned, however, it can be said that an ordinary support has become a work of art as it brings to mind in an unsurpassable manner the pulse of life which throbs in the marble in its perpetual pathway from bottom to top, the force which withstands the weight, simply the life which ennervates the lifeless stone. Furthermore, all the columns slant inwards, the corner ones, indeed, in a double movement, as much on the long side as on the narrow. For if the columns were completely perpendicular the upper sectors of the temple would appear to open outwards, as we observe so often in modern buildings where the vertical sections maintain their perpendicularity along their entire length. Parallel with this permutation of columns and dimensions (where through imperceptible differences the monotony of lifeless repetition is avoided) the freedom and beauty of rythmic breathing was ensured.

The majority of the refinements were not new. They had been known to Greek architecture for some time and it had striven to perfect them, to achieve an even more spiritual expression of them. In the Parthenon, however, like everything else, they have reached their crowning moment, one step further and their covert tension is extinguished, the variants lost, the forms deadened. As always perfection comes before the end, so it is with the Parthenon, the most Classical of all the monuments of antiquity, it precedes Classicism.

Sculpted decoration of the Parthenon

The sculpted decoration covered every available surface, every part of the building amenable to such embellishment within the limits which Greek sensitivity permitted. The traditional decorative 'grounds', the metopes and pediments all received, without exception sculpted decoration. Pheidias — who was also the principal coordinator of the decoration programme, even though he delegated its execution to several of the best artists in the country and even to select ones from further afield — borrowed an element from the Ionic order, the frieze, with which he surrounded the external face of the upper part of the main building behind the *peristasis* (colonnade). Thus the Doric canons were preserved on the outside. The *metopes,* which were the first members to receive decoration, were worked on between 447 and 442 B.C. Their artists still kept the superb somatic vigour of the so-called Severe Style of the previous generation, in variations corresponding to the number of artists Pheidias' presence is discernible. In the subjects, however, the "programme" and purpose of the whole work is apparent. When the metopes of the E side present the Gigantomachy, that is the struggle between gods and giants, those of the N side the Fall of Troy to the Achaean Greeks, those of the W the Amazonomachy, that is the victorious campaign of the Athenians against the Amazons from the East, and these of the S side (which are the best-preserved, most of them are in the British Museum, one of them the SW, is 'in situ') the Centauromachy, that is the fight between the Thessalian people, the Lapiths and the wild equiform Centaurs — then this indicates the creator's intention quite clearly. He wished to register symbolically the most recent victorious campaign of Greece against the barbarians of the Orient or, perhaps, more generally of order and a disciplined people's triumph over unbridled forces. It was not the first time the Greeks had portrayed these

35. NW corner of the Parthenon.
36. Reconstruction of the W face of the Parthenon by the Prof. A. Orlandos.
37. The W face of the Parthenon as it is today.

36

37

38. The NE corner of the Parthenon (the sculptures of the pediment are replicas of the
originals which are in the British Museum).
39. Reconstruction of the E face of the Parthenon (the central scene of the pediment is
of unknown composition)· (drawing by Professor Orlandos).
40. The E face of the Parthenon as it is today.

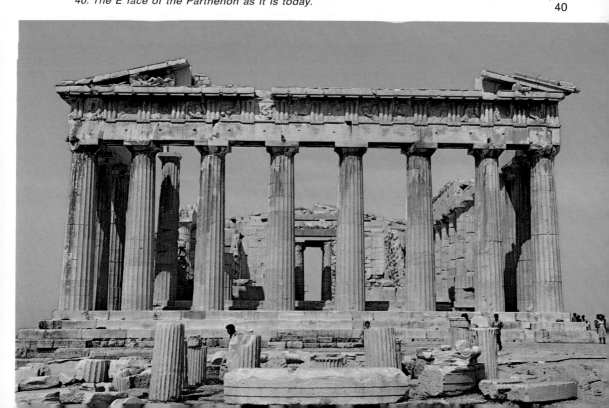

themes from their myths, however, here the symbolism was obvious and studied.

On the frieze, which was made in about 440 B.C., the personality of Pheidias has wholly dominated the team with its greatness of inspiration. The subject, taken from the life of Athens, is the representation of the procession of the *Great Panathenaia,* during which the whole city offered the peplos woven by the *Arrephores* to the goddess. From this enormous work of art, the total length of which was 160 metres, the greater part (apart, of course, from that destroyed in the explosion of 1687) is in the British Museum while various sections are in the Acropolis and other Museums while the entire west side is still in place on the building. This side shows the departure of the procession (it commences at the NW corner of the building), the handsome *ephebes* (-young men) who wait in line to mount their splendid steeds and later, when they are already astride them, they gallop away to catch up with the streaming procession. More will be said of the frieze later in the chapter of the Museum.

Last in chronological order were the pediments (438-432 B.C.) and of these first the east and afterwards the west one. Only top-class sculptors worked on both of them, and into both of them the sculptors put all their efforts, their work are perhaps the most wonderful ever to emerge from a sculptor's chisel, figures which take one's breath away and 'blow one's mind'. The figures here are not in relief but in the round, statues independent of their background, a whole world of their own which expresses, there on high, not as before in the indirect language of the relief but in the immediacy of remarkable plastic art. Moreover, the symbolism of the scenes depicted on the pediments is deep. However, we shall leave this subject for later since we shall speak in greater detail of the sculptures exhibited in the Museum. Nowadays virtually none of the very few figures still to be seen on the pediments is original, neither the blissful, indolently reclining Dionysos at the left edge of the east pediment and the superb horse's head at the right edge (the originals are in the British Museum) nor the tender group of Kekrops and his daughters which we see on the west pediment (the original is in the Acropolis Museum).

The cult statue of Athena, work of Pheidias

The plastic prolificity of Pheidias did not end with this immense wealth of figures for, naturally, the main sculpted work in the temple was the colossal cult statue of Athena Parthenos which stood in the depths of the cella, fashioned of ivory and gold. The principal features of the work are known from Pausanias' description and some small later copies (the best-known is the "Barbakeion Athena" in the National Museum). Standing, holding the Nike in her extended right hand and with the spear on her left shoulder and the shield resting below, beside her left foot, wearing on her head a helmet with a most unusual plumed adornment, the goddess amalgamated in this statue her two aspects, the polemic and the pacific. Besides the impressiveness of her stance and her general brilliance, the Parthenos of Pheidias was the most perfect expression of the enlightened yet ready for everything, Athenian democracy of Pericles. All that has survived of this work today are a few stones from its base which was also embellished with reliefs showing the birth of Pandora. The subsequent history of the statue is uncertain. Was it destroyed in the conflagration when the Herulae, as has recently been suggested, took over not only Athens but the Acropolis as well in 267 A.D.? Or perhaps, as scholars have tended to suppose, assuming that the Herulae did not capture the Acropolis at all but only the lower city, Pheidias' masterpiece was removed, according to one author from the close of antiquity, the 5th century A.D., most probably to be transferred to Constantinople?

41. The S pteron of the Parthenon.

42. The interior of the Parthenon as one sees it from the NE corner facing westwards.

43. A perspective reconstruction of the Parthenon by the Academician Professor A. Orlandos.

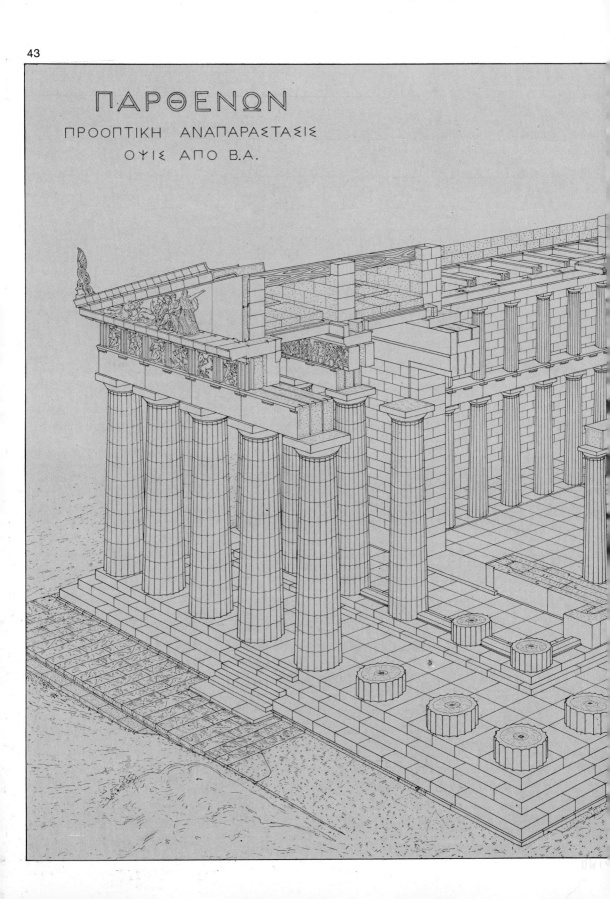

ΠΑΡΘΕΝΩΝ

ΠΡΟΟΠΤΙΚΗ ΑΝΑΠΑΡΑΣΤΑΣΙΣ

ΟΨΙΣ ΑΠΟ Β.Α.

ΑΘΗΝΑΙ 1948

44. The interior of the Parthenon as one sees it from the height of the west cornice and facing eastwards.

The Parthenon as the place in which the public exchequer was kept safe

The back of the temple served an important role for the city. For here was stored the public fortune, the exchange of Athena as it was called, and the treasuries of other deities as well, of the city and the countryside. This is not a surprising fact, by depositing public monies inside their temples the ancient cities ensured its sacred custody. In olden days the treasury of Athena was, as we shall see, kept in the "Old Temple". The Parthenon undertook to continue this duty as early as 439 B.C. as an inscription verifies.

The Parthenon as a church

In the 5th century A.D. the Parthenon became a church dedicated to Aghia Sophia (Holy Wisdom) (like the prototype of the great church in the capital of Byzantium Constantinople). Minor alterations made to facilitate the new mode of worhip, such as for example, the addition of an apse to the eastern part, caused damage and it was perhaps then that the central

The Parthenon as a Muslim mosque

complex of figures on the east pediment (if not earlier by zealous Christians) were destroyed. From this period originate the painted medallions of saints which were still visible until a few years ago on the inner part of the west wall of the temple (they have meanwhile disappeared). The Franks, who conquered Athens in 1205, naturally consecrated the church to the Latin dogma and the Turks did likewise following their capture of Athens in 1456 when the building was dedicated to the faith of Islam. Until the 17th century the building maintained, despite its many adventures, its architecture intact as well as the major part of its sculpted decoration. The catastrophe occured in 1687 when, during the war between the Venetians and the Turks, the former, under General Morosini besieged the Turks on the Acropolis and bombarded it with their canons on the surrounding hills. It is difficult for us to comprehend why the Turks had decided at that time to store quantities of gunpowder in the building which was their main mosque, maybe because there was plenty of space available there since the other buildings of the stronghold were occupied. Anyway, as one of the shells struck the building on 26/9/1687 the gunpowder blew up with great violence causing the destruction of a large part of the building and grievous losses to the sculpted decoration. After the explosion came the desecration of the corpse. At the beginning of the 19th century His Bretannic Majesty's Ambassador to the court of Constantinople, Lord Elgin, favoured by the particularly cordial relations between his country and the Sublime Porte succeeded in being issued with a Sultanic firman (1801) which allowed him to remove as many antiquities as he wished from the lands of friendly Turkey. Aided by the Italian sculptor Lugieri he removed, over a ten-year period, a large part of the sculpted decoration of the Parthenon as well as, at some other time, one of the Karyatides from the Erechtheion and various architectural members from these buildings and several other antiquities. The sale of this incredible treasure to the British Museum in 1816 was the culmination of this operation which gave the personage of Elgin much greater fame than his non-existent diplomatic activities.

Destruction of the Parthenon (1687)

Misappropriation of the sculptures of the Parthenon by Lord Elgin

As the visitor proceeds from the Parthenon towards the Museum his glance will inevitably fall for a short while on the ruins of a small monument with foundations of conglomerate stone, not poros-stone as in the other buildings of the Acropolis, while the entire upper structure is of Pentelic marble. From its shape it is quite clear that it dates from Roman times: round and with an Ionic colonnade which simply supported its conical roof without a room. This elegant type (called *monopteros*) was much beloved in Roman Imperial times and a large well-preserved inscription engraved on the epistyle validates, in the manner of the era, the year when the building was inaugurated (27 B.C. when a certain Areos was Archon of Athens) and the divinities worhipped therein (the goddess Roma and the god-Emperor Augustus). Worthy of special attention are the capitals, the hypotrachyle being astonishingly similar to those of the Erechtheion for imitation and even workmanship betray one of the main tendencies in the art of that period, Classicism.

Temple of Roma and Augustus

We will deal with the Museum in a separate chapter even though a visit to it comes chronologically after the visit to the temple of Roma and Augustus. Just for the information, I note two further points of interest located in the Museum area: The first is the shrine of the hero and mythical king Pandhion which came to light in excavation and is nowadays preserved in the Museum basement, the second is an outstanding section of the Mycenaean (Cyclopean) fortification wall which stretches out behind, that is east of, the Museum.

Sanctuary of the hero Pandion

A few metres north of the temple of Roma and Augustus, at the point where the rock reaches its maximum height (156 metres above sea level) the cuts preserved permit the location of an important sanctuary on the ancient Acropolis which has now disappeared, the shrine of Zeus Polieus. The restoration of the form of the temple is due to the American archaeologist Stevens. The very strange cult, the crux of which was the slaughter of an ox, is described in detail by Pausanias as well as by an author from the close of antiquity.

Sanctuary of Zeus Polieus

Between the Parthenon and the Erechtheion anyone with a modicum of experience, the will and the patience, may decipher the traces of the foundations of a very important building. His task would be much simpler if the foundations were all of the same material, but they are not. For, on the one hand their nucleus is of greyish-blue limestone like that of the Acropolis,

"Old Temple"

ΑΝΑΠΑΡΑΣΤΑΣΙΣ ΤΟΥ ΧΡΥΣΕΛΕΦΑΝΤΙΝΟΥ ΑΓΑΛΜΑΤΟΣ
ΠΡΟΣΘΙΑ ΟΨΙΣ

45. Reconstruction of the chryselephantine statue of Athena of Pheidias which was in the cella of the Parthenon (drawing by Professor Orlandos).

though it may very well have come from some other hill in the vicinity since the geological composition is the same, the surrounding foundation, however, is of poros-stone, the softer rock which is found in Piraeus and elsewhere. The building which stood on this foundation was the holiest on the Acropolis, it was the one which contained — at least prior to the construction of the Erechtheion adjacent — the exceedingly venerable statue of the goddess Athena, a wooden idol of such primitive form that it was said to have fallen in most ancient times from heaven (*diipetés*) and had not been fashioned by human hand. To it were addressed the honours of the devout and, apparently, it was this which was clad in the famous *peplos* even after the Parthenon, which housed the brilliant chryselephantine statue of Pheidias, had been built. The temple bore the name of Athena Polias, frequently, however, particularly in the Classical period, it was commonly referred to periphrastically as the 'Old Temple'. Its foundations are not, of course, so old as to merit this name since they are dated (they either belong to two periods as

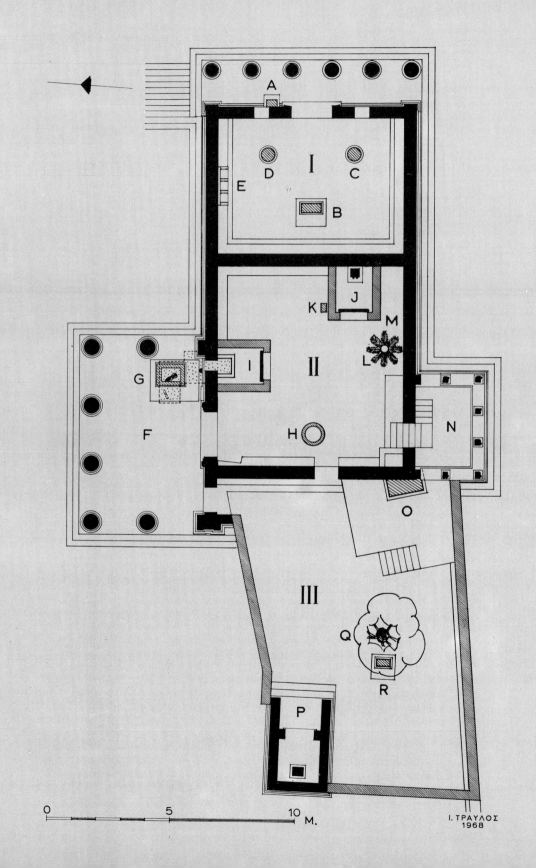

I. ΤΡΑΥΛΟΣ
1968

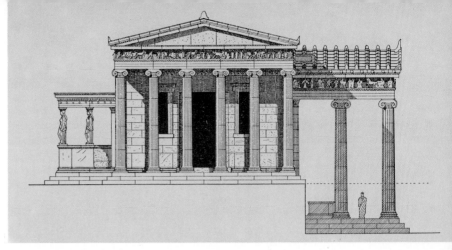

47

48

46. Reconstruction plan of the Erechtheion and Pandroseion according to the architect J. Travlos. The division and arrangement of the interior of the Erechtheion are new proposals of his.

47. Reconstruction plan of the E face of the Erechtheion (after Stevens).

48. Part of the W face of the Erechtheion and the olive tree which was planted in modern times in place of the ancient one.

49. The porch of the Karyatides from the SE (1978).

was formerly believed, or to one) to the 6th century B.C. and there was no other temple on the Acropolis deserving of this name. The reason is, then, that previous temples had existed on the same spot. Neither their number nor the date of the initial one can be determined. Their existence is betrayed by just a few but clear finds. Thus, the two poros-stone bases one sees a few metres to the south of the Erechtheion, encircled reverently with railings by the Archaeological Service, must originate from the wooden columns of the prodomus of one of the early temples. The same applies to a copper *elasma* (sheet) nowadays exhibited in the National Museum, which shows a Gorgon and must have been the acroterium of one of these precursors. These temples would have been small and their material perishable — the major part of the walls would have been of unbaked bricks though the roof decoration must have been of fired clay and painted in many colours. The votives must have been rich to deserve Homer's appellation of one of its predecessors "strong dwelling of Erechtheios" (shining) or "wealthy temple", «Ἐρεχθῆος πυκινὸς δόμος» or «πίων νηός». Worship took place with the sacrifice of oxen on a large altar situated to the east of the building. For this far-off temple was not only dedicated to Athena but to Erechtheus or Erechthonios, a most ancient god who with the passage of the centuries was thought to have reigned over Athens at some time. This cohabitation was also maintained by the temple of which we see the foundations and to which we now return. If we pay attention it will become clear that the main building has two sections, an east and a west. The first has the typical triple length-wise division and was considered to have belonged to Athena, the second, the west, is separated into three rooms and was believed to have belonged to the male god. However, by this time Erechtheus had been relegated to obscurity and Poseidon was the male deity with whom Erechtheus was often merged, Ionic god of earthquakes and the sea who violently swept into the pantheon of Attic religion and contested with Athena, according to tradition, for the sovereignty of Attica. He withdrew finally vanquished and compromised with her, casting, meanwhile, Erechtheus from his domain. Indeed, according to one tradition he slew him with his trident (according to another Erechtheus was killed by Zeus' thunderbolt). Nevertheless, Erechtheus never actually lost his personality and eventually succeeded in giving his name to the building, as well as to the later building which replaced it at the end of the 5th century B.C. (Erechtheion). Since the discovery of this very holy relic of Attic religious belief in 1866 there has been a continuous discussion among archaeologists concerning the form of its roof and primarily, the decoration it bore at the end of the 6th century. Here, however, is not the place to assess the various opinions, a very general outline will be given in the chapter on the Museum since the sculpted decoration is exhibited there. Here we confine ourselves to mentioning that in around 520 B.C. this temple was, for reasons unknown, repaired fundamentally, keeping the same dimensions yet including more recent architectural elements with more copious use of marble which was also extended to the pediments. Initiators of this work were, as we have already said in the historical note, the Peisistradides. The destruction of the building by the Persians in 480 B.C. did not signify its end. The west sector was repaired and re-used both for worship and for the safeguarding of the public exchequer (that is until the era of the Parthenon). Neither was the accidental (?) fire of 406 B.C. the final blow for there are indications that the building continued to thrive for several decades more. Its end was just as silent as its beginning, the building at some time simply slipped out of historical consciousness and the traveller Pausanias, who was writing about the middle

of the 2nd century A.D., did not describe it at all, not merely because he did not see it but because he had never even heard of it.

In 420 B.C. the temple which was called the Erechtheion began to be built right beside the "Old Temple" which it was destined to replace. Its shape is extremely complicated and presents several deviations from that of other Greek temples. A primary significant idiosyncrasy is the fact that it is built on two levels. Another is that it has two "prostaseis" (porches) on its west sector, one on the NW side and one on the SW. These and other peculiarities are explicable if we bear in mind that the unknown architect had to unite in a single building, or at least take into account in his design, the considerable ipsometric difference in the ground as well as the presence of several earlier shrines and holy spots mainly from cults of a mysterious nature.

The temple was divided into two. The east part was consecrated to Athena Polias, that is the old pacific goddess of agricultural Athens who was first worhipped in the adjacent temple. This sector is appreciably higher than the west which was dedicated to Poseidon-Erechtheus. It is not known whether there was any communication between the two sectors.

Let us commence our visit to the temple from the east. It has the usual type of entrance with six lovely Ionic columns (the last on the right is missing, it is in the British Museum). On looking at the interior today, the visitor sees nothing more than a uniform area wherein it is virtually impossible to distinguish where, in antiquity, the temple of Athena ended and the temple of Poseidon began. Moreover, the confusion is compounded by the fact that the ruins of the inside do not come solely from the ancient building but also from the Christian church into which the temple was transformed, seemingly in the 7th century, drastically altering the ancient situation.

In antiquity the east sector, the temple of Athena, housed the rudimentary-looking, but extremely holy, cult statue of the goddess of olive wood which was said, according to tradition, to have fallen from the sky (diipetés).

This sacrosanct idol was attired by the faithful in raiment and adorned with genuine precious jewellery.

Equally, if not more so, sacred for the ancient Greeks was the west sector of the temple, that which was dedicated to Poseidon. Here the Athenians pointed out the signs of the quarrel between Poseidon and Athena. To reach this sector we must first descend a staircase beside the north fortification wall (the staircase is modern though one did exist here in antiquity which occupied the entire width as far as the temple). We find ourselves in a courtyard where the altar of Zeus Hypatos stood. Opposite us stands a magnificent gateway (propylon) formed of 6 Ionic columns arranged in the form of a Π, leading to the shrine of Poseidon. There is an opening in its marble floor which allows us to see the holes which, according to the ancient Greeks, were made by Poseidon's trident when he struck the rock with all his strength, when he disputed with Athena. In olden times the hole was surrounded by an altar via which the holy signs received the libations of the faithful.

If we now raise our heads to the ceiling we will see that there too is an aperture indicating the direction which the god's trident followed. According to tradition, when the trident struck the rock a spring of sea water gushed forth, the element of which Poseidon was overlord. One could see this water somewhere inside the Erechtheion. If we stop awhile at the great north portal of the Erechtheion and look towards the interior there is a kind of cistern in front of us. Although its plaster lining is much later it seems that on this very

50. *The SE corner of the Erechtheion (1978).*

51. *The SE corner of the porch of the Karyatides (1978).*

spot was also the source of salt water "the Erechtheian sea" («ἡ Ἐρεχθηῒς θάλασσα»), which, according to Pausanias roared on the days when there was a south wind, just like the real sea. The cistern was subterranean, above it was the marble floor of the water which is nowadays missing. In the inner reaches of this chamber were the altars of Hephaistos and an early hero Boutos, on the walls were murals.

All these have been lost to us for which reason I shall limit myself to describing what we can see. The workmanship of the columns of the north propylon is worthy of admiration. The Ionic capitals here are much richer than on the Nike temple and the Propylaia. There is an additional zone of floral ornaments underneath which, in antiquity, were painted in colours.

Everything here points to the fact that we are no longer in the Severe period of the Parthenon but in the refined years of the close of the Civil Peloponnesian War, in the time of Alcibiades. Also well-known is the grand doorway with its rich decoration. Nowhere, however, does the lavishness intrude on the impression of tranquil equilibrium, the finesse is not transformed into affectation. It is true that the entire lintel is a subsequent Roman replacement of the initial Classical one which was damaged by fire but even on the copy one can distinguish the virtues of the original.

In the contest for the occupation of Attica, as we have said, Athena was triumphant. She struck the rock with her spear, according to tradition and an olive tree appeared, the silver-green Mediterranean tree with its blessed fruit. There is an olive tree on this spot today, just outside the west portal. It was planted by Queen Sophia on the site where the ancient olive tree of Athena must have stood. The Persians burnt it in 480 B.C. — but miraculously — it sprouted up the very next day, so the ancient Greeks said. The area to the west of the building was the humble, in comparison with the Erechtheion, sanctuary of Pandrosos, an Athenian nymph of cool places who was closely affiliated to Erechtheas.

In the SW corner again, underneath the Karyatides, where there is a modern hypostyle the ancient Greeks pointed to the tomb of the mythical king Kekrops, father of Pandrosos.

Porch of the Karyatides

The large wall visible here, orientated E-W, belongs to the "Old Temple" of Athena which was burnt by the Persians. If we climb up to the same level we are able to admire the unforgettable Karyatides; six lithe maidens which appear to support the cornice of a charming little prostasis on their head. They face the Parthenon and the route followed by the great procession of the Panathenaia which wended its way to the entrance of the Parthenon in order to deliver the peplos of Athena. Work of one of the pupils of Pheidias (usually said to be Alkamenes) the Karyatides are unsurpassed as an expression of maidenly femininity and uninhibited haughtiness and are admirably associated with the building of which they constitute support. One of them, (the second from the left of the façade) is a copy of the original which is part of the Elgin Collection in the British Museum while the last one on the right, the sixth, is for its greater part a free imitation in marble by an Italian sculptor of the last century because the original had been lost (part of it was found again a few years ago). Today the problem of replacing the originals with copies must be faced. It is necessary to remove them to a Museum in order to protect their surface from corrosion caused by sulphur in the atmosphere. The arms of the Karyatides are missing, it is, however, most probable that the left one held the robe and the right one some other object. The head does not support the cornice directly but through a carved 'basket'. There was another sculpted decoration on the Erechtheion, the frieze which surrounds the building and the N porch (there was none on the porch of the Karyatides). The technique was an innovation for the period: the Pentelic marble figures were affixed to the background of dark Eleusinian marble. Not one of them has survived 'in situ', many which have been found in excavations are now in the Acropolis Museum. Their number is not sufficient for us to decipher the subject and synthesis though it almost certainly presented old Athenian myths.

Before we conclude our visit to the Erechtheion it is a good idea to pause for a short time in front of the south wall in order to admire the beautiful band (*taenia*) which crowns the uppermost part, beneath the frieze (*epicranitis*) and displays a lovely alternating series of flowers and calyxes.

52. The theatre of Dionysos on the S slope of the Acropolis as seen from the rock.

Inscription of Gaia

Returning once more in the direction of the Parthenon, there are two further places of interest where we should stop. At a distance of 26,50 m. from the NW corner is an inscription of Roman times, fenced off, carved on the rock "Fructiforous Gaia according to the oracle" *(«Γῆς καρποφόρου κατὰ μαντείαν»)*. Next to it is a small levelled area indicating that here stood a statue of Gaia, from her waist upward, that is as if emerging from the rock. Further east, along the length of the north side of the Parthenon, is a row of Roman wells.

A final glance at the Parthenon. A robust, plastic mass full of vigour and beauty. Opposite it the Erechtheion, small and delicate beneath the Attic sky. Yet both of them are distinguished by the perfect clarity of their lines, the plasticity of their mass, their serene placement within the area.

A few words about the later fate of the Erechtheion. In early Medieval times it became a church. It was then that the interior completely lost its ancient form. In the Frankish period it became a Commandery, under the Turks it was the Governor's harem. During the struggle for Independence it suffered considerable damage. It was restored at the turn of the century.

Building material incorporated into the N fortification wall

The rampart of the Acropolis passes very close to the north part of the Erechtheion. At this point the manner in which the wall is built is so strange that it must surely surprise the unsuspecting visitor. For it consists for an appreciable part of its length and height of half-worked column drums of Pentelic marble. These are the drums from the columns of the Preparthenon which was not actually completed when it was destroyed by the Persians in 480 B.C. After the return of the Athenians to their homeland these were incorporated in the fortification wall as a reminder to the Athenians, who gazed on the sacred rock from the Agora, of the sacrilegious deeds of the barbarians. This was done either by Themistocles, who fortified Athens, or a few years later by Kimon who, according to a specific testimony of Plutarch, initiated the construction of the south rampart of the Acropolis.

These are not the only architectural members to have been incorporated in the north fortification wall of the Acropolis. Slightly further west, built into the north rampart is a row of members from the upper structure of another temple of the Acropolis, the "Old Temple" of Athena. These are only visible if one views the Acropolis from the outside. They are poros-stone triglyphs, marble metopes and a poros-stone cornice, all placed in the order they occupied on the building.

Place where kores were found

To the NW of the Erechtheion is an open pit in which were found, during the excavations of 1886 most of the Archaic kores which are the boast of the Acropolis Museum. They must have stood somewhere in this area before they were destroyed by Xerxes' army in the summer of 480 B.C. Many of them perhaps portray specific persons (priestesses?). When the Athenians returned home vistorious they collected them together reverently and buried them here to sleep, as they believed, their immortal sleep. Nowadays they have been brought back to life and fill the Archaic galleries of the Museum with their radiant smile of youth. It is significant that the ancient Greeks made no attempt to repair and re-erect them as we would have done today. For them the statues were not Museum pieces but more like a relic of beloved people, be it of marble or of bronze, was just as alive as man himself. (This is made clear to us by the inscriptions written in the first person, that is as if the statue itself was speaking).

Arrephorion

There were also some small buildings on the inner face of the fortification wall in this area. Of these the one nearest the Erechtheion and of which the poros-stone foundations are clearly discernible was a small house in the shape of a temple 'en parastasis', the so-called Arrephorion. This was the dwelling of the Arrephores, the young girls who wove the peplos of Athena for the Panathenaia and who participated in a strange ritual which took place once a year on a summer night. The Arrephores then received from the priestess of Athena a sealed canister which they were forbidden to open and passing via a secret exit they carried it down to the sanctuary fo Aphrodite below the Acropolis on the NE foothills of the rock. From here they took another similar canister without opening it this time either and without knowing what they were carrying.

Another ancillary building for the cults of the Acropolis stood at the west edge of the north slope towards the Propylaia. It was of simple form. These buildings looked towards the inside of the sanctuary, towards the "inner courtyard" as the American archaeologist Stevens has characteristically called it. This area, as we have already said, was crowded with 'ex-votos' many of which were works of famous artists. Amidst them predominated, on

Statue of Athena Promachos

account of its size, the colossal bronze statue of Promachos Athena, also a work of Pheidias, whose spear glistened as far as the sea, signal of warmth and security for the souls of the Athenians who took the road to foreign parts, mirthful invitation to those returning to their beloved home.

53. *The hind wall of the Stoa of Eumenes on the S slope of the Acropolis. In the background the hill of the Muses and the monument of Philopappos.*

54. *The Herodeion as it appears from the Acropolis.*

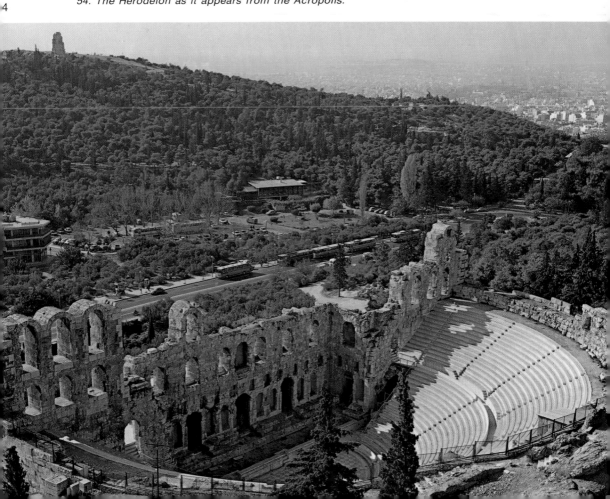

THE ACROPOLIS MUSEUM

Reorganised after the Second World War by the Ephor of Antiquities Yannis Miliadhes, the Acropolis Museum is one of the most important in the world. If Greek art is one of the peaks in the progress of world art and if sculpture constitutes perhaps the most typical expression of the Greek artistic genius then the Acropolis museum has the rare privilege of containing almost exclusively masterpieces from the centuries of the great acme of ancient Hellenism from its principal artistic centre, Athens, dedicated to its most famous sanctuary, the precinct of Athena Polias. So the tour of the galleries of the Acropolis museum immediately after visiting the monuments constitutes, for every art lover, a unique and unrepeatable experience.

There are two periods of Greek art which are glorified on the Acropolis, the Archaic and the Classical. The first is represented in uninterrupted sequence and unique quality from its first monumental beginnings until the moment it is mixed with Classical art. By strange good fortune disaster salvaged this precious bequest for us. In 480 B.C. this entire treasure was demolished from its place, broken and shattered by the Persians who occupied Athens for a short period of time. When the Athenians returned shortly afterwards, victorious, the ruins were buried with reverence in hollows in the rock (the so-called "Persian stratum" of the excavation) where they remained forgotten for centuries, thus avoiding the disasters and thefts which subsequently laid waste the Acropolis. The Classical votives had not the same luck. Very important statues of bronze and marble, works of the best-known artists of antiquity have been lost forever and their existence is only known from the precious description of the traveller Pausanias (middle of the 2nd century A.D.) and their presence on the rock is attested only by the cuttings which received their bases. Fortunately, however, several of the sculptures which adorned the monuments have survived from this period. Most of these have been nefariously taken abroad, mainly to England, to the British Museum, of which they comprise one of its best-known collections (the Elgin Marbles), part of them are still 'in situ' on the monument, and others are on display in the Acropolis Museum.

Before entering the museum we are confronted by a tall pedestal on which sits the owl, the sacred bird of Athena who watches us with its big round eyes (500 B.C. no. **1347**).

Vestibule:

In the vestibule, opposite the entrance, stands a 5th century B.C. group which is attributed to the sculptor Alkamenes, pupil of Pheidias. The mythical queen of Thrace and daughter of the king of Athens, Prokne who contemplates the murder of her son Itys to avenge the unfaithfulness of her husband. Not the horrible act, but the tragic conflict taking place in the mother's soul and the bitter irony which impels the unsuspecting but disturbed child to cling to his mother, seeking her "protection", has been rendered by the artist, according to the custom of the 5th century. These as well as the severe and sparse magnificence remind one of Classical tragedy.

Gallery I:

The visit to the galleries begins from the left. In the first gallery works of around 600 B.C. and from the early years of the 6th century B.C. are exhibited. This was the era of Solon, the great reformer of the Athenian state, society and legislature. During these years building activity on the Acropolis was feverish. Temples large and small were dedicated to Polias Athena, patroness of the city and to other gods and local heroes. Their pediments were decorated with relief scenes, either of demonic beasts of Anatolian inspiration or imaginary monsters or, finally, mythological scenes. Indeed, myth predominated particularly on the pediments of the smaller temples and gradually took precedence on the larger ones, displacing the animals and monsters. The rendering of these sculptures, works of inspired imagination, their simple yet powerful style, the incredible confidence in the use of the chisel which the carving displays indicate that the Athenian sculptors of thoses times were creators of art of a high quality. Particularly impressive is the monumental composition of a lioness killing a calf (no. **4**). It comes from the pediment of a large temple of circa 600 B.C., perhaps the first post-Geometric phase of the so-called "Old Temple" of Athena Polias of which we see the ruins to the south of the Erechtheion. The subject is oriental and apparently has an 'apotropaic' significance. Here, however, thanks to the strong personality of the Athenian artist, it has been stripped of the conventionalism of eastern art and been transmuted into an artistic creation of the highest merit. Next to it is another pediment, much smaller though, coming from a little temple or treasury. On this is portrayed, in bas-relief, Herakles struggling to overcome the polycephalous Hydra while his friend, Iolas, (no. **1**) awaits him in his chariot. The ancient colours, plain but strong (red and deep blue) are very well preserved. Opposite is a marble Gorgon of which the head and only a small part of the body have survived (no. **701**). It was the acroterium of a large temple, of the beginning of the 6th century B.C., most probably of the second phase of the "Old Temple" mentioned previously. From the frieze of the same building are the sections of panthers exhibited to the left of the entrance (no. **552, 554**) and the head of a panther near the entrance to the second gallery (no. **122**). From the porous cornice of the same temple comes the fragment with the incised and painted lotus blossom near the entrance (no. **4572**).

Gallery II:

The sculptures in the second gallery also date from the first half of the 6th century B.C. To the right, on the long wall, are exhibited sculptures from one of the two pediments of the afore-mentioned temple, to the second phase. A supple-bodied Herakles wrestles with the Triton, a sea demon (no. **36**) half man, half fish, while at the other edge is a winged three-bodied demon with a serpent's tail (no. **35**). Each of the three demons holds a symbol in its hands, water, fire and a bird (symbol of the air). This is Nereas, demon of the watery element who was continually changing shape. Worthy of attention is the expression on the faces which not only are not in the least terrifying or demonic but, on the contrary, give an impression, unknown in the Orient, of humanity, something one comes across from now onwards in every Greek creation. Also to be noticed is the simple but vigorous residuum of the masses which are carved by deep, decisive incisions wherever details are registered or also finely-worked relief bends, the whole with copious but obvious use of colours (dark blue and red).

The narrative style of the period is admirably represented by the pediment of the deification of Herakles on Olympus (no. **27-29**). Zeus majestically seated on his throne with Hera at his side received the mighty hero on Olympus. The details of the garments, the thrones etc. are highly refined and discreetly adapted to the whole. The large snakes which are displayed above the window are from the decoration of the rear frieze of the large temple. Despite the schematisation beloved in that period the execution of the slithering heavy body which simultaneously swayed in its elevation from the earth (no. **37, 40**) is quite wonderful.

One of the first most important votives in the sanctuary was the statue of the Moschophoros (570 B.C.) (no. **624**) which stands in the middle of the gallery. According to the inscription on its base it was offered by a certain Romvos with piety, certainly a noble man from the countryside, who is here portrayed advancing joyfully to proffer his calf to the goddess. Eyes full of light and a deeply human smile give life to his innocent face while the head of the calf is turned towards his own. During these years marble began to be used for ex-votos. At first it was brought from nearby Hymettos but soon it was also brought from Paros whose quarries were renowned for their milkish-white translucent marble (lychnites). For instance, a standing and smiling sphinx facing the centre of the gallery is of this type of marble (no. **630**).

At almost the same time another kind of votive made its appearance and was later to predominate; these were the statues of young maidens, the so-called *kores.* What do they really represent? Even though their faces seem to have individualistic features they do not necessarily depict specific persons nor are they necessarily exclusively and solely female votives. Their significance is more general; they are simply "statues", (Greek ἄγαλμα from the verb ἀγάλλομαι = to rejoice) that is votives which brought pleasure to the goddess who was evidently more delighted with these offerings than with any other. The earliest of the kores is that which stands behind the Moschophoros (no. **593**), immobile, like a solid mass which, however, has been rendered with great feeling by the hand of a sensitive artist.

Gallery III:

In the next gallery are two other kores, one from Samos (no. **619**) and the other from Naxos (no. **677**), rather cold and expressionless. Alongside them a magnificent composition attracts one's attention and takes one's breath away; two lions lacerate a bull (no. **3**). They occupied the centre of the same pediment on which Herakles and the Triton as well as the three-bodied demon in the preceding gallery occupied the two corners. The subject is of the same quality as that in the first gallery but differs in that this composition, being later than the other, is less constricted, less heraldic, the bodies are more realistic and the movement faster and more violent, the realism almost raw.

Gallery IV:

The fourth gallery contains marble sculptures from the second half of the 6th century B.C. For the greater part of this century Athens was ruled by Tyrants, first the genius Peisistratos until his death in 527 B.C., afterwards his sons Hippias and Hipparchos. Only during the later years of the century was tyranny superceded by democracy. Even though the tyrants ruled with force in their city they were, at the same time, interested in the arts and poetry and undertook the construction of many temples and other public edifices. Under Peisistratos the votive statues on the Acropolis continued to multiply and Athens became the number one centre of the arts in the entire Hellenic world.

The Horseman which confronts us as we enter comprised part of a votive (560-550 B.C.) (no. **590**). Initially the work consisted of two equestrian figures alongside one another which perhaps represented the sons of Peisistratos. The archaic rigidity is combined with the finely chiselled coiffure like embroidery, while an unsurpassed graciousness, purely Attic, diffuses from its form. It is known as the Rampin horseman from the name of the French collector who owned its head before it passed into the Louvre collection in Paris (here there is a plaster-of-Paris copy of the original). Next to the Rampin horseman stands the statue of a kore, usually referred to as the Peplophoros (no. **679**) on account of the peplos, a simple unpleated garment of Doric provenance which she is wearing. Superior, with its phenomenally rigid stance, radiant face, eyes full of light, finely chiseled face, this work of circa 525 B.C. must have come from the chisel of a great artist of the era, perhaps the same as fashioned the horseman.

To the same artist are attributed also other works such as the hunting dog nearby (no. **143**) which is presumed to have guarded the entrance to the sanctuary of Brauronian Artemis and the lion head a little further on (no. **69**), on the wall, which was surely used as a water-spout on the "Old Temple" which the sons of Peisistratos rebuilt in honour of Athena in around 525 B.C. (3rd post-Geometric phase).

The small relief, no. **702,** perhaps shows Nymphs led by Hermes and followed by the dedicator; it is charming in its simplistic freshness, a folk work in which the Nymphs face the spectator fully while dancing towards the left.

The horseman with the strange attire, barbarian trousers painted with strong colours (no. **606**) may have been the Tyrant of Thrace, Miltiadhes. His horse is monumental and heavy. A second horse which is behind the dog (no. **70**) is slightly later (end of 6th century), sinewy, agile and lively.

The kore which stands next to the horseman (540 B.C.) (no. **269**) is markedly Ionic, both in its dress and in its rather rotund body. The greater part of the body and the head is a cast of the original which is in Lyon, France and from where the statue takes its name "kore of Lyon". In the same gallery, but on the opposite side, a very 'petite' kore is also Ionic or Ionic-like (no. **675**) elegant and resplendent with its rich colours, especially alluring with its sweet smile. It seems to be the work of a certain artist from Chios where sculpture at that time flourished.

The head (no. **643**) affixed to the wall is clearly an Attic work but the execution of the flesh and the smile achieve the epitome of femininity which the chisel of the artists of this very refined period were capable of. Similarly feigned, almost pretentious, is the headless kore (no. **594**) and the body of Theseus (no. **145**) with the exceptionally sensitive, almost tender, modelling.

Nevertheless, in the final years of that century the fashion for beautiful, graceful and very elegant draperies with many pleats, very fine outlines, radiant visage and feminine smile began to die out. The head (no. **696**) which is located behind head no. **643** displays, one might say, a wanness of form, as if a shadow had fallen over the eyes, as if it stares at the inner world. It is dated to around 500 B.C. as is kore no. **674**, the most interesting of them all, which stands festively, formally, within the semicircle opposite it. The smile is retained only at the corners of the lips and the facial expression is seemingly frozen at a passing thought. This is the first time the figure acquires self-awareness, the moment when man achieves full appreciation of his limits, of his destiny and of himself. The era of tragedy has been born.

The first kore in the semicircle (no. **684**), ten years later, as it stands robust and square, seems to correspond perfectly with the picture we have formed of the women of the heroic generation of Marathon. Its face is, nevertheless, slightly cold and expressionless. Its artist simply imitates the work of the artist of the preceding one.

A large seated Athena (no. **625**), nimble and seemingly ready to leap up from her seat, presides over the company; it is apparently a work of the great sculptor Endoios. It is also one of the very few works which escaped destruction when the Persians took over the Acropolis in 480 B.C. Pausanias refers to it among the other votives he saw on the Acropolis (2nd century A.D.).

Gallery V:

In the following gallery, opposite, larger-than-life marble figures (no. **631**) which adorned the pediment of the temple which the sons of Peisistratos had consecrated to Athena (3rd phase of the "Old Temple") dominate. It represents the battle of the Olympian gods with the Giants and even though Zeus was present, Athena occupied a central position on the pediment just as she also dominated the hearts of the pious Athenians. Here we see her huge, launching into battle with a wide stride, allowing her terrifying aegis with its snakes to billow as she stoops over an opponent (of which only the leg has survived) to deliver the fatal blow. Another giant, its enormous body wracked with pain, has fallen nearby. Two more giants, kneeling at the two extremes of the pediment, gather strength from their mother Gaia to also launch into the battle.

In the same gallery, on the right, is the largest kore of all (no. **681**), votive of the potter Nearchos as the inscription on the base which is displayed beside it informs us and work of the famous sculptor Antenoros. Broad-chested, monumental, this is the most "Attic" of all the kores of the Acropolis. It rather tends to impose itself on the visitor than the others which win him over with their attractive familiarity. In the corresponding position to the left of the entrance to the gallery is another equally tall, considerably damaged kore (no. **1360**) which exhibits the traits of an island (Parian?) artist: meticulous attention to details, yet obvious lack of feeling for the organic skeleton.

Alcove:

The cases at the far end of the gallery contain some small marble sculptures and other objects originating from the Acropolis and vases which were found in the excavations conducted to the south of the Acropolis between the years 1955 and 1961. Noteworthy is the "pyxis" with geometric decoration from a tomb of the beginning of the 8th century (1961 - NAK **301**), vase handles with incised votive inscriptions (graffiti) to an unamed Nymph, fragment of a black-figured vase with a representation of a marvellous horse and others.

Gallery VI:

The next gallery is not very big and does not contain many sculptures. However, they are included amongst the most important creations in the whole of Hellenic art. They saw the light in a glorious period, at the time when the Greeks received the terrible blow of the Persian onslaught which they met with the fearlessness of despair at first, and with the invincible force which the drunkeness of victory brings, subsequently. The body and face of the ephebe which faces us on entering (no. **698**), certainly the victor in some contest, effuse pride and greatness. The Archaic conception of the suporting of the body on both feet has been abandoned here: the right limb has been freed, the body turned to the same side as the inclined head (Classical counter-balance "contra posto") the expression is serious, Classical art commences with the "Severe style". The statue is known as "Kritios' Ephebe" because it was chiselled by Kritios, teacher of Myron.

The youthful head which we see nearby and on which traces of golden-yellow colour on its hair (Blonde ephebe) are still preserved (no. **689**) is the work of another artist. With a melancholic, almost dolorous expression it turns sideways. Its body, as its pelvis exhibited opposite indicates, has the Classical stance like that of the Ephebe of Kritios. To youths such as this, Athens owed not only its victory at Salamis but also the tremendous floruit of subsequent years.

The relief of Athena who leans on her spear with her head inclined pensively (no. **695**) is one of the most famous and yet most unpretentious works. It has an aura of finesse, sensitivity and austerity.

One should pay particular attention to the kore dedicated by Euthydikos (no. **686**), to the right of its inscribed base with the lower part of its body (no. **609**) known as "Boudeuse" (490 B.C.) on account of its morose expression. The details have been rendered with extreme clarity so much so that they belie an inclination to imitate bronze works which began to increase during that period. The wonderful horse before us (no. **697**) which seems to whinny is perhaps the most beautiful horse created by Greek art before Pheidias. Next to it is the body of a nude ephebe of 490 B.C. (no. **692**), tender work of an island artist. And further on, a pensive, almost melancholic head (no. **699**) contemporary with the Parthenon, remarkable work of one of Pheidias' colleagues.

Gallery VII:

What Athens and the Parthenon were in Pericles' day was said by Pericles in his funerary oration, delivered in honour of the dead in the first year of the Peloponnesian War, in a few words which, rightly, have been famous ever since. In all its aspects it represented an incredible acme of the Greek intellect the virtues of which were, apparently all concentrated in an unparalelled manner in the Parthenon. The greatest names of Greek art, headed by the greatest genius of them all, Pheidias, worked at that time to laud the glory of Athens and of Athena. As Plutarch narrates, Pheidias was the one who thought of everything, who took care of all. Certainly the majority of the sculptures which embellished the Parthenon were made by other artists who were pupils of his. On all, however, is stamped the seal of Pheidias' genius and he, most probably, made the designs. Metopes, frieze and pediments comprised a trilogy which remained 'new' for all time. Even the most insignificant fragment, combining material and spirit in its purest form, makes one's heart beat quicker every time one sees it. From these pieces are assembled here the tender composition of Kekrops and his daughter from the west pediment and, next to it, the body of Poseidon (no. **885**), gigantic, reclining, truly titanic, also from the west pediment, further on, Selene driving her horses to the setting of the moon (no. **881**) from the east one, the Centaur trying to seize a Lapith (no. **705**), from a metope, heads of whinnying horses (nos. **882, 884**), a proud virginal head, Iris from the west frieze (**855**) et al.

Gallery VIII:

In this spacious gallery are displayed numerous sections of three of the friezes which embellished the large buildings of the Acropolis in the 5th century B.C.: of the Parthenon, the Erectheion and the parapet of the Wingless Victory. The majority are plaques from the Parthenon frieze which depicted, as we have said already in the chapter on the Parthenon, the procession of the festival of the Panathenaia (circa 440 B.C.). Even though they constitute only one very small part of the initial whole which surrounded the building for a length of 160 metres, they create quite an impression, especially all along the long wall where the plaques from the north side are exhibited. Youths, wearing sunhats or wreaths surge forth along with the rich wave (no. **868, 862** etc.), youths getting in and out of chariots (no. **859**), "hydriaphoroi" (pitcher-bearers) (no. **864**), "thallophoroi" (no. **865**), youths guiding rams (no. **860**) or oxen to sacrifice (no. **857**), all in closely-knit or dispersed groups move in an uninterrupted and rhythmic flow towards the east side where, unseen by them sit the gods of Olympus, talking casually amongst themselves or casting a glance (no. **856**: Poseidon, Apollo, Artemis, Aphrodite) in the direction of the central scene where the peplos is being handed over (British Museum). The faces of all, whether mortals or gods, are serious and introverted even when the forms are interconnected by the movements. Moreover, nowhere are specific persons portrayed, the features of all are idealised. Similarly, no specific landscape has been registered, the procession unfolds against a neutral, idealised background. And yet the wave of people and the galloping horses have been rendered with unique conviction, the successive levels of the dense shapes have been denoted with unrepeatable mastery. The artist who undertook this great work, who sketched at least in general outline, who perhaps executed the prototypes for some of the critical scenes, cannot have been other than Pheidias himself to whom is due the conception as well as the responsibility for the entire plastic decoration of the monument. But here also, as we have already said, the execution of the work was assigned to a host of sculptors which one may separate without much difficulty and some of which, who are distinguishable on account of their superb plastic ability, are none other than his close collaborators whose names we know from literary tradition: Alkamenes (perhaps the artist of the plaque of the gods no. **856**), Agorakritos etc.

The second frieze represented by fragments of it in Gallery VIII is that of the Erechtheion. On the small partition wall in the middle of the gallery,

Miliadhes displayed certain choice pieces of it in the same way as on the monument. The figures did not protrude in relief from the body of the frieze but consisted of separate pieces of white marble which were attached to the background of the frieze which was of another material — black Eleusinian marble. Although the subject is not certain it is probable that old Athenian myths were portrayed. In these sculptures, which belong to the second phase of work on the Erechtheion (409 - 406 B.C.) one observes that the movements of the figures and the fall of the draperies is much heavier and the divine current which pervades the Parthenon frieze from end to end is absent. Furthermore, the artists of whom a few are known to us from an inscription, were not the top ones of the era.

Further on, at the edge of the gallery, are the plaques comprising the parapet of the Nike tower (circa 415 B.C.). Athena and Nike adorn, in numerous combinations, these plaques. Five or six artists chiselled these plaques, as one can easily recognise. Most of the artists were first class but, alas, anonymous. However, it is more than likely that one of them was the famous 'katatexitechnos' (that is he who mastered his art with his fine workmanship) Kallimachos. Which, however, of them? Maybe the one who carved plaque **972** in which two Nikes push an ox for sacrifice, their raiment turbulent from the effort. Or perhaps he who worked on plaque **973** in which a dazzlingly youthful Nike unloosens her sandal while her himation clings to her beautiful body as if wet?

Gallery IX:

The rapid deterioration of the condition of the Karyatides of the Erechtheion by the sulphur content of the atmosphere of Athens in recent years has obliged the Greek state to remove them to this gallery of the Acropolis museum and replace them on the monument with copies. By the time the reader is reading these lines the originals may already be in this gallery, inside an air-conditioned chamber with constant temperature. Even though the display is not satisfactory it is unavoidable and only possible one considering present conditions.

In the same gallery some sculpture from the old gallery have been kept. I mention two. One is the head of Alexander (no. **1331**) of which the characteristics are more or less depersonalised, almost divine, work perhaps of the sculptor Leochares who portrayed the Macedonian king on the occasion of his only visit to Athens after his great victory at Chaironeia (338 B.C.). Very characteristic of its period the gentle moulding which diminishes the sharpness of the features (sfumato in Italian) and the deep eyes which endow the expression with pathos. The other sculpture is the head of a wreathed old man with long beard and long hair (no. **1313**). He belongs to a world entirely different from the world of Alexander as with his wide open eyes he seems to gaze steadfastly on worlds far off which his fiery soul wishes to reach. His eyes betray a mystic and but for the wreath they could belong to some Christian. However, we have here one of the last teachers of the Neoplatonic system of philosophy which, at the close of antiquity, brought Plato very close to Christianity. The skilfulness and, even more so, the plastic and expressive force of the Athenian artist are astonishing. In front of this great work which was created on the threshold of the Middle Ages, a thousand years after the Archaic lioness, at the very last moment before the death of the world of idolatry, we cannot but feel yet again deep admiration for the Athenian genius.

55. *Statue of Prokne studying the killing of her son Itys. Perhaps a work of the sculptor Alkamenes, pupil of Pheidias (440 B.C.).*

56. *Part of the base of a statue dedicated by the leader of the chorus, Atarvos, in memory of his victory in a contest.*

57. *Base of a statue decorated with relief representation of the "dismounting" contest (end of 4th century B.C.).*

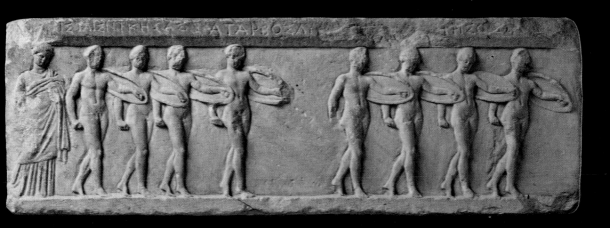

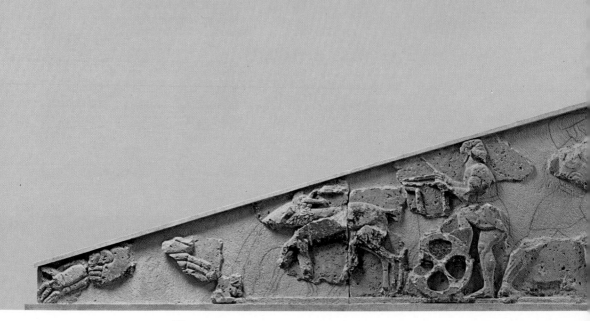

58

59

58. Poros pediment of
Hydra (from a small temple
or treasury of the beginning
of the 6th century B.C.).

59. Head of a marble
Gorgon. The Gorgon was
the acroterium of a large
temple from the beginning
of the 6th century B.C.,
perhaps of the "Old
Temple" of Athena.

60. Lioness killing a cow.
From the decoration of the
pediment of a large poros
temple of circa 600 B.C.

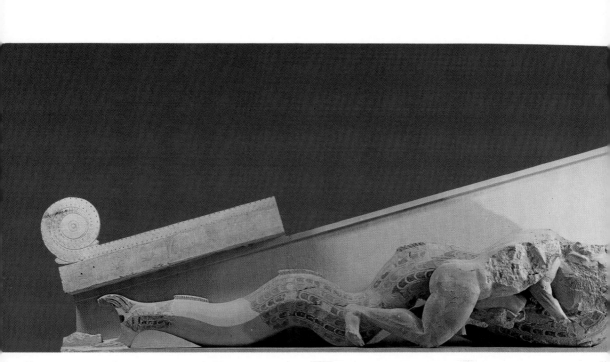

61

61-62. The two extremeties of the composition of the pediment from a large temple of the beginning of the 6th century B.C., perhaps the "Old Temple" of Athena (see plate 59). On the left Herakles wrestling with a sea demon, on the right a three-bodied demon, an embodiment of the forces of nature (water, fire, earth).

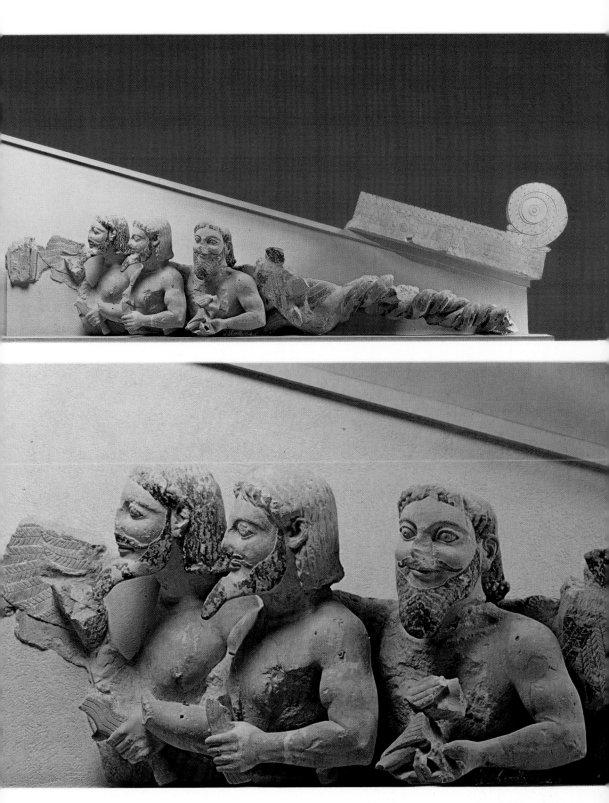

63

64

63. Superbly vital poros snake from pediment 59-62.

64. Part of a smaller poros pediment of about the same age which depicts Herakles' (on the right) entry into Olympus.

65. The "Moschophoros", statue of the patriot Romvos (from the inscription on the base) who offers the sacrificial calf to Athena (570 B.C.).

66

67

66. *Marble sphinx (560 B.C.).*

67. *Marble quadriga, 'ex voto' of 570 B.C.*

68. Marble sphinx of 540 B.C.

69. Two lions killing a bull - poros composition from the centre of the pediment of the "Old Temple" the edges of which were embellished with the compositions in plate 61.

70. Reconstruction plan of the above composition.

69

ANAΠAPASTASIS / RESTORATION

71. Marble kore, the so-called "peplophoros", masterpiece of 530 B.C. (traces of colour).

72. Equestrian statue known by the name of the "Rampin Horseman" after the French collector who at one time was in possession of the head (nowadays in the Louvre - a plaster-of-Paris copy is in the Acropolis Museum). Another masterpiece of 560 B.C.

ΚΑΛΛΙΚΟΜΟΙ ΚΟVΡΑΙ ΔΙΟS ΛΡΧΗSΑΝΤ ΕΛΑΦΡΩS

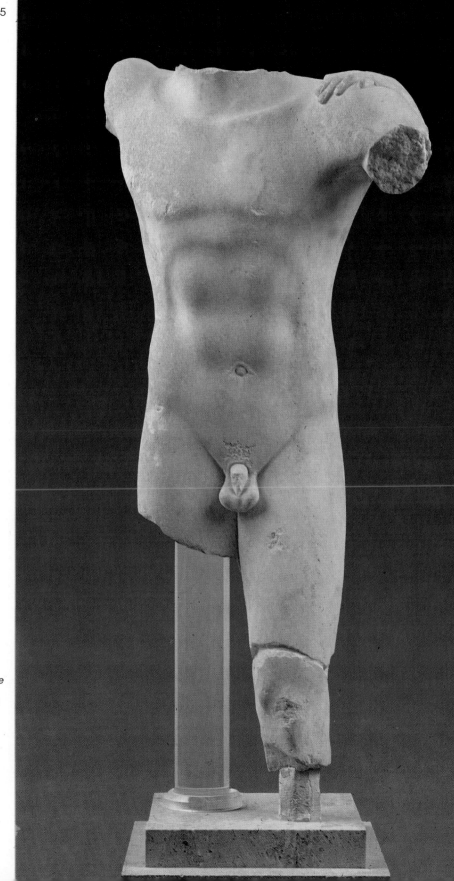

73. Delightful marble votive relief depicting Hermes, perhaps Nymphs and the dedicator(?) (circa 510 B.C.).

74. Exceptionally lifelike marble dog (from the Brauroneion?) 530-520 B.C.

75. Surprisingly sensitive statue of a naked youth wrestling with an opponent (see the hand on the left shoulder). Perhaps Theseas. 520 B.C.

76. Marble kore of 510
B.C. with vivid colours.
Work of a Chian artist.

77. Marble kore of 510
B.C. with richly draped
garments on which
much of the colour is
preserved.

78. Marble head of a kore from the end of the 6th century B.C. with the beginnings of introspective expression.

79. Marble head of a kore of 510 B.C. with supple fleshy curves, femininity and marked Archaic smile.

80. Marble equestrian statue of 510 B.C. Lithe construction, proud movement.

81-82. One of the most important kores, masterpiece of 500 B.C. in which the expression begins to be introverted and the smile is preserved only at the corner of the lips, imparting an enigmatic air to the face.

82

83a. Marble kore of 490 B.C.

83b. Marble kore of 500 B.C.

84. Marble relief, perhaps from the frieze of the "Old Temple" as it was renovated by the Peisistratides in 525 B.C. It represents one of the gods energetically mounting his chariot.

85. Marble kore of 510 B.C.

86. Marble kore of 520 B.C.

87. Marble kore of 520 B.C. on which much of the colour is preserved.

88. Marble kore of 510 B.C. with traces of colour.

89. Tall marble kore of 520 B.C. influenced by the art of Chios. Many of the colours are preserved.

90. Flying Nike. Island work of 500 B.C. Colours preserved.

91

91. Large marble Athena from the pediment of the Gigantomachy of the "Old Temple",
as it was renovated in 525 B.C. by the Peisistratides.

92. Athena and an injured giant from the pediment of the Gigantomachy.

93. One of the giants from the same pediment - the right edge.

94. Marble head of an
Ionian kore of 510 B.C.

95. The head of a marble
kore of 510 B.C., perhaps of
Peloponnesian
workmanship.

96. The largest of the
marble kores, work of 520
B.C. If the base in plate 97
belongs to it then it is the
work of the famous sculptor
Antinoros.

97. Base of a kore with
incised inscription
referring to the potter
Nearchos as its dedicator
and the sculptor Antenoros.
Attributed to the kore in
plate 96.

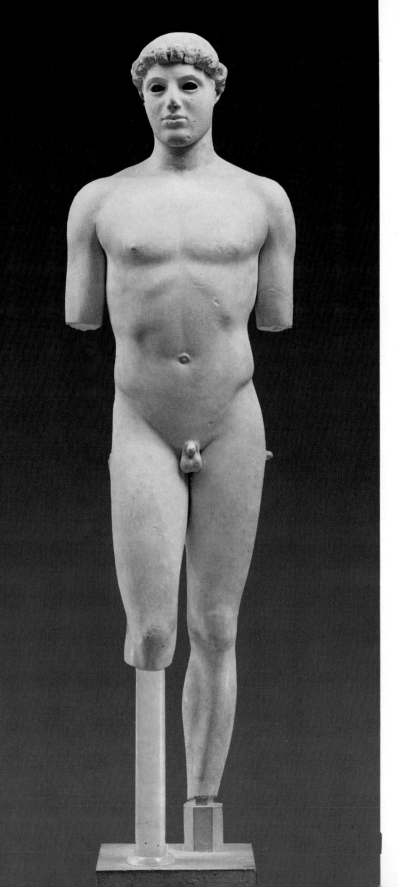

98. *Very beautiful marble statue of an ephebe athlete. Work of 480 B.C. which is attributed to the sculptor Kritios, the teacher of Myron.*

99. *Head of the "Ephebe of Kritios".*

100-101. *Head of a marble statue, the so-called "Blond Boy". Masterpiece of 480 B.C., perhaps of the teacher of Pheidias.*

100

101

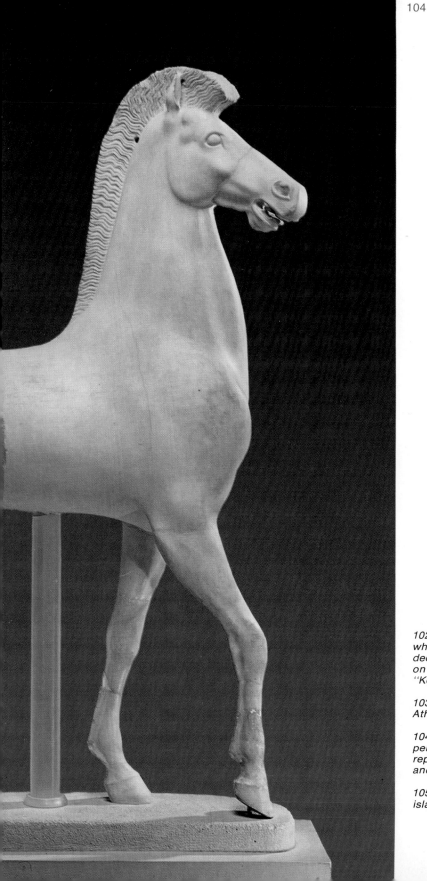

102. Marble kore of 490 B.C.
which, after the name of the
dedicator which is preserved
on its base is usually called
"Kore of Euthydikos".

103. Votive relief of "Pensive
Athena" work of 460 B.C.

104. Marble horse of 490 B.C.,
perhaps the most inspired
representation of a horse in
ancient art.

105. Marble body of an ephebe,
island art. 490 B.C.

106. From the Parthenon frieze (440 B.C.)

107. Head of a victorious athlete of 440 B.C.

108. From the Parthenon frieze. Head of Iris.

107

108

109. Metope of the Parthenon (440 B.C.). Centaur seizing a Lapith.

110. Kekrops and his daughter. Sculpted marble composition from the west pediment of the Parthenon (circa 435 B.C.)

110

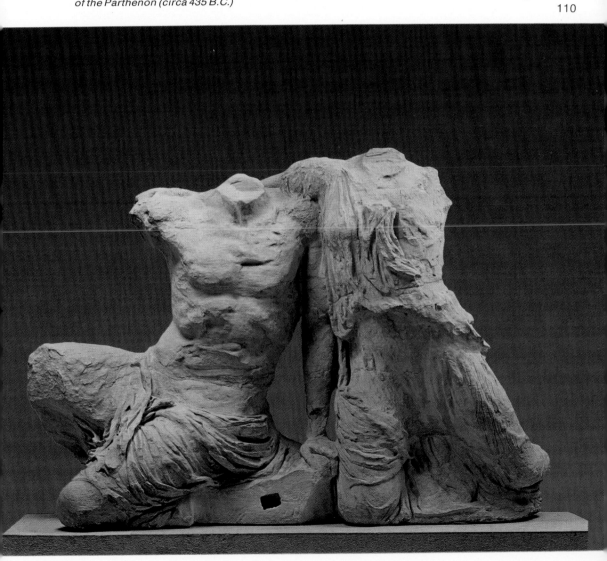

111. From the Parthenon frieze. Young pitcher-bearers (hydriaphoroi).

112. Detail of a pitcher-bearer.

113. Plaque from the Parthenon frieze. Men in discussion.

114. From the Parthenon frieze. Young men leading oxen for sacrifice.

115. From the Parthenon frieze. Horsemen.

116. From the Parthenon frieze. Young men leading rams for sacrifice.

117. From the east frieze of the Parthenon. Gods. From the left: Poseidon, Apollo, Artemis.

118. Detail of Artemis.

14

15

119. *From the parapet of the Nike temple. Nike leading an ox for sacrifice (415-410 B.C.).*

120. *From the parapet of the Nike temple. Nike unloosing her sandal.*

121. *Head of Alexander. Work of Leochares(?).*

122. *Head of a Neoplatonic philosopher (5th century A.D.).*

THE ACROPOLIS AND ITS MONUMENTS

1. Approach of Classical times.

2. Pedestal of Agrippa (earlier of Eumenes II).

3. Propylaia.

4. Nike temple.

5. Brauroneion.

6. Chalkotheke.

7. Parthenon.

8. Temple of Roma and Augustus.

9. Sanctuary of Pandion.

10. Sanctuary of Zeus Polieus.

11. Altar of Athena.

12. Erechtheion.

13. Pandroseion.

14. Arrephorion.

15. Statue of Athena Promachos.

16. Klepsydra.

17. Panathenaic Way.